Emil Bretschneider

**Archaeological and Historical Researches
on Peking and Its Environs**

Bretschneider, Emil: Archaeological and Historical Researches on Peking and Its Environs
Hamburg, SEVERUS Verlag 2011.
Nachdruck der Originalausgabe von 1876.

ISBN: 978-3-86347-164-4
Druck: SEVERUS Verlag, Hamburg 2011

Der SEVERUS Verlag ist ein Imprint der Diplomica Verlag GmbH.

Bibliografische Information der Deutschen Nationalbibliothek:
Die Deutsche Nationalbibliothek verzeichnet diese Publikation in der Deutschen Nationalbibliografie; detaillierte bibliografische Daten sind im Internet über http://dnb.d-nb.de abrufbar.

© **SEVERUS Verlag**
http://www.severus-verlag.de, Hamburg 2011
Printed in Germany
Alle Rechte vorbehalten.

Der SEVERUS Verlag übernimmt keine juristische Verantwortung oder irgendeine Haftung für evtl. fehlerhafte Angaben und deren Folgen.

ARCHÆOLOGICAL

AND

HISTORICAL RESEARCHES

ON

PEKING AND ITS ENVIRONS.

By E. Bretschneider, M. D.

ALMOST all the celebrated capitals of the ancient kingdoms in Europe, western Asia and India, have been the subject of more or less extensive critical investigation by European antiquaries, and bulky works have been published relating to these matters. But with respect to China our scholars seem to be quite ignorant as to the remains of this ancient civilization; and even regarding Peking, one of the best-known places of the Middle Kingdom, and its classical soil, very little is known. The archæologist, who would devote himself to the investigation of the antiquities of China, finds considerable aid in Chinese literature. The Chinese have always had a taste for antiquities, and those of past ages have been careful to leave to posterity, records of remarkable facts, not only in books, but also in inscriptions on stone tablets. During the terrible wars which have successively ravaged China in the past, many of these ancient monuments, so important for archæology, have naturally disappeared; but copies of a great number of ancient Chinese inscriptions have been preserved in native archæological and other books. No nation in the world has ever paid so much attention to its history, geography and antiquity as the Chinese. In China, every district possesses special works, devoted to the most detailed description of it, as regards the political changes during several tens of centuries, the geographical configuration, the products and other accounts. These descriptions comprise often a large number of volumes. One or several chapters are always devoted to the 古蹟 *ku tsi* or "ancient vestiges."

As regards Peking, which has been for so long a time the capital of China, the works devoted to its description have been numerous in former times; but very few of these ancient accounts have come down to us in a complete form. For the most part we can now only find fragments of them quoted in other works.

One of the most ancient descriptions of Peking existing, and relating to the 10th and 11th centuries of our era, is that found in the history of the *Liao dynasty*. A similar one is found in the history of the *Kin dynasty*, dating a century later. Besides these, two or three descriptions of ancient Peking have been left by Chinese travellers of that time. The *Yüan shi*, or "History of the Mongol dynasty" gives also a short description of the capital and the palaces built by Coubilai khan in the 13th century. A more detailed account of the Mongol palaces is contained in the *Ch'ue keng lu*, by a writer of the same dynasty, and in some other works of the 13th and 14th century, of which fragments have come down to us, and which I shall mention further on. Of the time of the *Ming* dynasty, 1368-1644, we possess several descriptions of Peking and its neighborhood. One of them is entitled 春明夢餘錄 *Ch'un ming meng yü lu*. Nobody would guess from this title, that the book is a description of Peking and its environs. *Ch'un-ming* was the name of a celebrated library. I would translate the title, "Accounts found in the *Ch'un-ming* library during intervals from sleep." The work contains 70 chapters. The name of the author is 孫承澤 *Sun Ch'eng-tse*. He lived in Peking in the first half of the 17th century. This is a very valuable work, giving many interesting accounts of ancient Peking.

The title of another work of about the same time reads 帝京景物略 *Ti king king wu lio*, or "Sketch of the remarkable things of the Imperial Capital." It was published in 1635 in 8 chapters.

A third ancient description of Peking to which I have access is the 長安客話 *Ch'ang an k'o hua* in 8 chapters, written about the close of the 16th century.

But all the above-mentioned books are superseded by the 日下舊聞 *Ji hia kèu wen*, which was first published by 朱彝尊 *Chu I-tsun* at the close of the 17th century, in 42 chapters. The meaning of the title is literally, "Ancient (accounts) heard under the sun (*i. e.* in the capital);" and the subject of the work is an archæological and historical description of the imperial precincts in Peking, and the twenty-six districts dependant on *Shun-t'ien fu*. A new, revised and much enlarged edition of it was published at the end of the last century, by imperial order, in 160 books. The character 考 *k'ao* (investigation) was added to the old title. In this work almost all that is found in Chinese literature regarding the history of Peking is brought together, and we find numerous quotations from ancient books, which do not exist at the present time. I shall give a short index of the *Ji hia kéu wen k'ao*[1]

Chap. i, 星土 *Sing-tu*, "Astrology."

Chap. ii-iv, 世紀 *Shi-ki*, "Ancient history of Peking and the country."

Chap. v-viii, 形勝 *Hing-sheng*, "On the beauties of Peking." Extracts from poetical compositions.

Chap. ix-xxviii, 國朝宮室 *Kwo-ch'ao kung-shi*, are devoted to the description of the palace building of the present dynasty; including eleven chapters on the palace proper, one on the 雍和宮 *Yung-ho kung* (the large lama monastery in Peking), and eight on the 西苑 *Si yüan*, or "Western park."

Chap. xxix-xxxvi, 宮室 *Kung-shi*, "Description of the palace" under the preceding dynasties. Chap. xxix gives an account of the palaces of the *Liao* and *Kin*; chap. xxx-xxxii, of that of the Mongol dynasty. Chap. xxxiii-xxxvi are devoted to the palace of the Ming, and the imperial parks, etc.

Chap. xxxvii, xxxviii, 京城總紀 *King-ch'eng tsung-ki*. These two chapters introduce the capital city in a general way.

Chap. xxxix-xlii, 皇城 *Huang ch'eng*, describe the "Imperial city."

Chap. xliii-lxi, 城市 *Ch'eng-shi*:—detailed description of the capital,—its temples and other remarkable buildings, streets, gates, etc. Twelve chapters are devoted to the "Tartar city" or 內城 *nei ch'eng*; seven chapters to the 外城 *wai ch'eng*, or Chinese city."

Chap. lxii-lxxiii, 官署 *Kwan-shu*, "The offices, tribunals, boards, etc." Chap. lxii, 宗人府 *Tsung-jen fu*, "Board for superintending the affairs of the imperial family." 內閣 *Nei-k'o*, "Grand Secretariat." 中書科 *Chung shu k'o*, "Department of Recorder for special and posthumous honours." Chap. lxiii, 吏部 *Li-pu*, "Board of civil office." 戶部 *Hu-pu*, Board of revenue." 禮部 *Li-pu* "Board of rites." 兵部 *Ping-pu*, Board of war." 刑部 *Hing-pu*, "Board of punishments." 工部 *Kung-pu* "Board of works." 理藩院 *Li-fan yüan*, "Office for foreign dependencies." 都察院 *Tu-ch'a yüan*, "Court of censorate." 通政使司 *T'ung-cheng shi-sze*, "Court for examining the reports from the provinces." 大理寺 *Ta-li sze* "Court of judicature."

Chap. lxiv, 太常寺 *T'ai-ch'ang sze*, "Court of religious ceremonial." 翰林院 *Han-lin yüan*, "National academy." 詹事府 *Chen-shi fu*, "Department having the supervision of the heir-apparent's studies."

---

[1]. As I shall frequently quote the *Ji hia kiu wen k'ao* in these papers, I will denote it for the sake of shortness, by *Ji hia*, and the *Ch'un ming meng yü lu* by *Ch'un ming*.

Chap. lxv, 光祿寺 *Kuang-lu sze*, "Banqueting court." 太僕寺 *T'ai-pu sze*, "Grand equerry's court." 順天府 *Shun-t'ien fu*. 鴻臚寺 *Hung-lu sze*, "State ceremonial department."

Chap. lxvi, lxvii, 國子監 *Kuo-tze kien*, "University." 文廟 *Wen miao*, "Confucian temple."

Chap. lxviii-lxx, 石鼓 *Shi-ku*, "Ancient stone drums."

Chap. lxxi, 欽天監 *Kin-t'ien kien*, "Board of Astronomy." 太醫院 *T'ai-i yüan*, "Medical College." 內務府 *Nei-wu fu*, "Imperial household."

Chap. lxxii, History of a number of military offices:—the imperial body-guard; the imperial equipage department; the eight banners; Van-guard brigade; Hunting-park brigade, etc.

Chap. lxxiv-lxxxvii, 國朝苑囿 *Kuo-ch'ao yüan-yu* "Imperial parks outside the capital." 南苑 *Nan-yüan* (or 南海子 *Nan-hai tze*), the vast enclosure south of Peking, is described in two chapters; 圓明園 *Yüan-ming yüan* in three chapters; 萬壽山 *Wan-shou shan* in one chapter; 玉泉山 *Yü-t'süan shan* (or 靜明園 *Tsing-ming yüan*) in one chapter; 香山 *Hiang shan* (or 靜宜園 *Tsing-i yüan*) in two chapters.

Chap. lxxxviii-cvii, 郊坰 *Kiao-k'iung*, "Suburbs and environs of Peking."

Chap. cviii-cxliv, 京畿 *King-ki*, "Description of twenty-six district cities dependant on the capital.

Chap. cxlv, 戶版 *Hu-pan*, "Accounts of the population."

Chap. cxlvi-cxlviii, 風俗 *Feng-su*, "Manners."

Chap. cxlix-cli, 物產 *Wu-ch'an*, "Products."

Chap. clii-cliv, 邊障 *Pien-chang*, "Fortifications of the frontier."—The great wall.

Chap. clv, clvi, 存疑 *Ts'un-i*, "Dubious questions."

Chap. clvii-clx, 雜綴 *Tsa chui*, "Miscellanies."

Besides the above-mentioned works, which at the present time are difficult to obtain, and the price of which is very great, there is a short description of Peking, entitled 宸垣識略 *Ch'en yüan chi lio*, published at the end of the last century. It is a useful book for reference and easily obtained. It has been partly translated by *Father Hyacinth* into Russian, and by *Ferry de Pigny* from Russian into French in 1829. This translation has been for a long time the only description of Peking known in Europe; from which all compilers have derived their accounts of the Chinese capital. A few years ago the Rev. *J. Edkins* published an article on Peking, as an appendix to Dr. Williamson's *Journeys in North China and Manchuria*. This is, without doubt, the best description of Peking we possess, and the best part of the book.

The learned author describes generally from personal observation, and adds a number of interesting historical notes.

In the following paper I by no means intend to give a complete account of the antiquities of Peking; and shall only select a few topics for review, and treat especially of such questions as are called for by the accounts of the great mediæval traveller Marco Polo, the first European who saw the Chinese capital.

HISTORY OF PEKING AND ITS NAMES AT DIFFERENT TIMES.

Peking, as Europeans call the modern metropolis of China, has been a capital and an imperial residence for more than nine hundred years. But long before this time it was an important place, often mentioned in Chinese history. The Chinese annals report, that in 1121 B. C. a descendant of the celebrated emperor *Huang-ti* was invested with a fief in the north, and that he resided at 薊 *Ki*,[2] which city is supposed by the Chinese to have been situated at about the same place where Peking now stands. During the *Ch'un-ts'iu* period, 723–481 B. C., and *Chan-kuo* period, 481–221, the city of *Ki* is mentioned as the capital of the kingdom of 燕 *Yen*, which for long centuries sustained an important rôle in the north of China. It was destroyed by *Shi huang-ti*, who, in 221 B. C. succeeded in uniting the whole of China in one empire. In the 4th century of our era, *Ki* was again the capital of a small realm governed by the Tartar house *Mu-jung*. After this for a long space of time, Peking is only mentioned in the histories of the dynasties which successively reigned in China, as a departmental city under the names of 薊 *Ki*, 燕 *Yen* or 幽州 *Yu-chou*. The name of Yen for Peking is used up to this time in books.

During the *T'ang* dynasty, 618–907, Peking was known under the name of 幽州 *Yu-chou*, and was the seat of a 大都督府 *Ta tu-tu fu* (military governor general).[3] In A. D. 936, Yu-chou was taken by the *Kitan* or *Liao*, who established their power in northern China, and was made one of their capitals under the name of 南京 *Nan king* (southern capital), called also 析津府 *Si-tsin fu* or 幽都府 *Yu-tu fu;* and since that time Peking has been, with short interruptions, the residence of the emperors of the Tartar, Mongol or Chinese dynasties, up to our days. In A. D. 1013 the name of the capital was changed to 燕京 *Yen king*. During the last years of the Liao dynasty, Peking was for a short time, 1122–1125, in the possession of the *Sung*, who reigned in

---

2. *Ki* must not be confounded with the present 薊州 *Ki-chou*, 180 *li* east of Peking, the name of which dates back only as far as the middle of the 8th century of our era. See the *Yi t'ung chi* or "Great geography of China."

3. As is known, the capital of the T'ang was 長安 *Ch'ang-an* (the present *Si-an fu* in Shensi).

middle and southern China, and they named the city 燕山府 Yen-shan fu.

In 1125, the *Kin* Tartars, after having destroyed the Liao dynasty, expelled the Sung from northern China; and in 1151 Peking became one of the residences of the Kin emperors, under the name of 中都 *Chung tu* (middle capital.), called also 大興府 *Ta-hing fu*. At that time already the capital was divided into the two district cities *Ta-hing hien* and *Wan-p'ing hien*, as at present.

In 1215 Tchinguiz khan took this capital of the Kin, and it was then for half a century only the capital of a Mongol province. But the conqueror's grandson, *Coubilaï khan*, transferred the residence of the Mongol emperors from Caracorum to Yen king in 1264; and in 1267 built a new city, which, from the year 1271, is called 大都 *Ta tu* (the great capital) in Chinese history; whilst to the Mongols it was known by the name of *Khanbaligh*.

In the year 1368 the *Ming* dynasty succeeded the Mongols, who withdrew to their native steppes. *Hung-wu* the first emperor of the Ming, 1368—1399, changed the name of the newly-conquered capital into 北平府 *Pei-p'ing fu*. In 1409 the emperor *Yung-le* left his capital 應天 *Ying-tien* or *Nanking* (southern capital) and established his court in *Pei-p'ing fu*, which name then was changed into 北京 *Pei-king* (northern capital). At the time the Jesuits first arrived in China, towards the end of the 16th century, this was the name in use to designate the Chinese metropolis. During the Ming, Peking, considered as a departmental city, bore the name 順天府 *Shun-t'ien fu*, and comprised two district cities, 大興縣 *Ta-hing hien* and 宛平縣 *Wan-p'ing hien*.

The Manchoo dynasty, which has reigned in China since 1644, did not change the names of the capital. I must however remark, that the name "Peking," so familiar to every European, is hardly known by the Chinese of our days. The learned Chinese understand of course what is meant by this name, but Peking is always called 京城 *King-ch'eng* or 京都 *King-tu*, both meaning capital, by the Chinese.

This is a summary of the history of Peking, which has seen so many political changes, and altered its name under almost every dynasty. We shall see, that the place, where the capital stood, has also changed several times.

The historical sketch of Peking, as given above, has been borrowed, for the greater part, from the *Yi t'ung chi*, the great geography of the empire; but all these historical accounts can also be found scattered in the *Ji hia*, and in other Chinese descriptions of Peking.

THE POSITION AND THE REMAINS OF ANCIENT PEKING.

I have not been able to find in Chinese books any statements about *Ki*, which point out the true position of this ancient capital. The old records however, although very vague, leave no doubt that it stood in nearly the same place where modern Peking is situated. There is a tradition, that the ancient rampart, 5 *li* north of Peking, belongs to the remains of *Ki;* and the emperor Kien-lung in the last century erected a monument near the north-western corner of this rampart, with an inscription and verses stating that here was one of the gates of ancient *Ki*. But as some of the Chinese authors are of opinion that the rampart north of Peking dates only from the time of the Mongols, I shall review these controversies further on, when speaking of the Mongol capital.

With respect to ancient *Yu-chou*, the name which Peking bore during the T'ang dynasty in the 8th and 9th centuries, its position can be more precisely indicated by monumental evidence. The *Ji hia* states (chap. xxxvii, fol. 18), that in 1681 an ancient tomb was dug up near the western gate of the imperial city (西安門 *Si-an men*), with a monument of the year A. D. 799, stating, amongst other things, that the place was distant 5 *li* to the north-east of *Yu-chou*. Another monument exists in the temple of 憫忠寺 *Min-chung sze*, stating that this temple, at the time it was founded, was situated in the south-western corner of *Yu-chou*. The temple of Min-chung sze, now called 法源寺 *Fa-yüan sze* was founded in A. D. 645. It lies in the western part of the Chinese city. (*Ji hia*, chap. xxxvii, fol. 18 ; chap. lx, fol. 1.)

In the history of the Liao dynasty (*Liao shi*, chap. xl) it is stated, that *Yen king*,—since the year 936 the southern capital of that dynasty (see above), was 36 *li* in circuit. The walls were 30 (Chinese) feet high, 15 feet broad, and throughout their whole extent provided with towers. The wall was pierced by eight gates. The names are enumerated. There were two on the north, two on the south, two on the west, and two on the east. The city was evidently a square. In the neighborhood of the capital are mentioned : the 燕山 *Yen-shan* (I do not know what hill is meant,—perhaps the western hills); the 高粱河 *Kao-liang ho* (a river. A bridge of this name still exists near the north-western corner of Peking); the 石子河 *Shi-tze ho* (the name of an ancient river west of present Peking, as I shall show further on. It does not now exist); the 桑乾河 *San-kan ho* (the river bears this name up to the present time. It is more commonly called *Hun ho* ;—see further on); the 居庸 *Kü-yung* (still the name of a fortress in a defile north of Peking); the 古北口 *Ku-pei k'ou* (still the name of an important defile in the north-east, leading from Peking to Mongolia).

Some other names of places, occurring in that ancient description of Peking, I am not prepared to identify. There are also some particulars regarding the palace of the Liao, situated in the south-western corner of the capital. Nothing in that description points to the position of the Liao capital.

There are two narratives of Chinese travellers preserved, who visited the capital of the Liao in the 11th and 12th centuries. In the year A. D. 1123, the *Sung* sent an envoy from 臨安府 *Lin-an fu* (the present *Hang-chou fu*, at that time the capital of the Sung), to 會寧府 *Hui-ning fu* near the *Sungari* river in Manchuria, to the court of the *Kin* (or *Djurdje*), which dynasty was just beginning to come to power. The complete itinerary of the envoy is found in the 大金國志 *Ta kin kuo chi*, chap. xl, under the title 許奉使行程錄 *Hü feng shi hing ch'eng lu*, or " Itinerary of the envoy *Hü*." It begins with 雄州 *Hiung chou*, where at that time, was the frontier between the Liao and the Sung.[4] The traveller gives the names and the distances of all the stations on his long route, and adds a number of interesting notes regarding the places he passed through.[5] He calls Peking 燕山府 *Yen-shan fu* (see above) and places it 30 *li* east of the 盧溝河 *Lu-kou ho* (*hun ho*), which river was crossed by him on a floating bridge; I am not able to say whether at the same place, where now the splendid *Lu-kou k'iao* stone bridge stands, or perhaps higher up the river. The Chinese now estimate the distance from the *Lu-kou* bridge to the *Chang-yi men* (western gate of the Chinese city) at 30 *li*. The next station mentioned by the traveller on his road to the east is 潞縣 *Lu hien*, 80 *li* distant from *Yen-shan fu*. According to the 太平寰宇記 *T'ai p'ing huan ya ki*, a Chinese geography of the 10th century (quoted in the *Ji hai*, chap. cvii, fol. 18), Lu hien was 30 *li* to the east of the *Lu* river, which is the ancient name for the 白河 *Pai ho*. At present the Pai ho (*T'ung chou*) is distant 40 *li* from the *Tung-pien* gate (near the north-east corner of the Chinese city of Peking). Therefore the eastern wall of Yen-shan fu must have been about 10 *li* west of the eastern wall of the present Chinese city.

Another Chinese traveller, also an envoy of the Sung, sent to Peking it seems in the 11th century (宋王會奉使錄景, see *Ch'un ming*, chap. vi, fol. 2) mentions the capital under the name of *Yu-chou*,

---

4. We learn from Chinese history, that in 1122, the *Kin* who were about to overthrow the *Liao*, agreed that the Sung should occupy the northern part of Chili and Shansi, belonging to the dominions of the Liao; and *Hü's* embassy to *Hui-ning fu* was evidently in connection with this transaction.

5. Some years ago, Archimandrite Palladius went from Peking to Manchuria by the same way as *Hü*. In comparing Palladius' itinerary with that of *Hü*, I found that almost all the places, rivers, mountains, etc. mentioned by the latter can be identified, and generally the names have not changed.

and states that *Liang-hiang hien* was distant from Yu-chou 60 *li*, and that between these cities he crossed the *Lu-kou ho* (see above). Liang-hiang hien is now estimated 60 *li* distant from the *Chang-yi* gate. This traveller gives also some accounts of the palace buildings of the Liao capital; but no deduction can be drawn from these statements, consisting in the enumeration of names only.

The history of the *Kin* dynasty (*Kin shi*, chap. xxiv), gives also some accounts of ancient Peking. It is stated there, that the *Kin* emperors enlarged the capital and called it *Chung-tu* (see above). Thirteen of its gates are enumerated. The Kin built a new palace, and the timber for the buildings was brought from 潭 圜 *T'an-yüan*, a park near *Cheng-ting fu* (more than 150 miles south-west of Peking). Besides the palace inside *Chung-tu*, some summer palaces and imperial gardens outside are mentioned; amongst others the 瓊 島 華 *K'iung-hua tao*, north of the capital. The same name is up to this time applied to a hill inside the precincts of the imperial palace. Thus the ground occupied by the modern Tartar city, was, at the time of the Kin, outside and north of the capital. Regarding the circuit of ancient Chung-tu, there are some discrepancies in the statements of the Chinese authors. The *Kin shi* does not give the figures of the circuit; the above-mentioned *Ta kin kuo chi* estimates it at 75 *li*, and states that the city had twelve gates. The same work records further, in describing the siege of Chung-tu by the Mongols, that it consisted properly of four walled cities, which the Mongols were obliged to storm separately. The circuit of 75 *li*, as given by the *Ta kin kuo chi*, seems too great, and the statement in the 太 祖 實 錄 *T'ai tsu shi lu*, or "Biography of the first Ming emperor Hung-wu (*Ji hia*, chap. xxxviii, fol. 11)" seems more reliable. In that work it is said, "the emperor gave orders to measure the 商 城 *Nan-ch'eng* (southern city). It was found to have a circuit of 53,280 Chinese feet (about 30 *li*). Nan-ch'eng at the time of the Mongols was the name of the ancient city of the Kin, the walls of which can still be seen (i. e. end of the 14th century. Compare also *Ji hia*, chap. ii, fol. 2)."

The *Ji hia* gives (chap. xxxvii, fol. 17,18) a very interesting review of the documents pointing to the position of ancient Peking, and refers generally to monuments with inscriptions found in ancient monasteries or on tombs, mentioning their position with respect to the capital at the time they were erected. There are a number of very ancient monasteries and pagodas in Peking and its neighborhood, some of them founded more than twelve centuries ago; and they generally have one or more tablets stating the time of their foundation and some particulars about it. The changes of the names are also mentioned. The greater part of such tablets do not exist at the present time, but their inscriptions have been preserved in archæological or other books. The following are the results of the investigations of the editors of the *Ji hia*.

"The ancient capital of the *Liao* and *Kin* was to the south of the present capital (i. e. Tartar city). At the time of the Yüan the walls still existed, and the ancient city of the Kin was commonly called *Nan-ch'eng* (southern city), whilst the Mongol capital was termed the northern city. As under the reign of *Kia-tsing* (middle of the 16th century) the 外羅城 *Wai-lo ch'eng* (which Europeans call the Chinese city) was built, the ancient traces disappeared, and it is impossible to distinguish the four sides. But if comparing critically the ancient inscriptions on monuments with what we see at the present day, we arrive at the following conclusions:

"For instance,—the monastery of *Min-chung sze*[6] is situated to the south of the 宣武 *Süan-wu* gate, not far from the 廣寧 *Kuang-ning* gate. The writers of the Mongol time record that this monastery was inside the Kin capital.

"There is a monastery 廣恩寺 *Kuang-en sze* now situated to the south-west of 白雲觀 *Po-yün kuan*.[7] It was called 奉福寺 *Feng-fu sze* at the time of the Liao and Kin. On the monument of *Tsao-kien*, dating from the time of *T'ai-ho*, 1201-1209, it is stated that the monastery was inside the capital.

"The temple, called 天王寺 *T'ien-wang sze* at the time of the Kin, is the same as 天寧寺 *T'ien-ning sze* of our days.[8] The *Yüan yi t'ung chi* (great geography of the Mongol empire) states that this temple was inside the Kin capital, in the quarter called 延慶坊 *Yen-king fang*.

"What is now called 琉璃廠 *Liu-li ch'ang*,[9] was at the time of the Liao, as has been proved by a monument dug up there, a village 海王村 *Hai-wang ts'un*, outside the eastern gate of Yen-king.

"West of the 先農壇 *Sien-nung t'an* (temple of agriculture) there is a brick-kiln called 黑窰廠 *Hei-yo ch'ang*. From the ancient monument of a Buddhist priest found near that place, we learn that at the time of the Liao it was situated to the east of the capital.

"The 北平圖經志書 *Pei p'ing t'u king chi shu* (a book compiled under Hung-wu the first Ming emperor) records, that the temple 土地廟 *T'u ti miao* was inside the ancient (Kin) city, south of the gate *T'ung-yüan men* (this gate was the second from the right of the four northern

---

6. Already mentioned; the same as 法源寺 *Fa-yüan sze*
7. *Po-yün kuan*, the temple where the Taouist monk *Ch'ang-ch'un* is buried. It was also inside the Kin capital (*Ji hia*, chap. xciv, fol. 1-3).
8. *T'ien-ning sze* was founded in the 6th century of our era. It lies between the *Chang-yi* gate and the north-west corner of the Chinese city, outside. It is well known for its beautiful pagoda.
9. The name of a street to the south-west of the *Cheng-yang men* or *Ts'ien men* gate.

gates of the Kin capital: see *Kin shi*). Now this temple is situated (in the Chinese city) to the south-west of the *Süan-wu* gate in the street called *Tu-ti-miao sie-kie*.

"It may be concluded from these statements, that the capitals of the Liao and the Kin both stretched west from the present *wai-ch'eng* (Chinese city) over the land now comprising the (western) suburbs, and that the north-eastern corner of these ancient capitals was about the place where now the tower of the south-western corner of the capital (Tartar city) stands.

"王煇 *Wang Hui* (an officer of the Mongol time) records in his work 中堂事記 *Chung t'ang shi ki*, that in the year 1260, in the 3rd month, proceeding from *Yen-king* to *K'ai-p'ing fu*,[10] he passed the first night in the suburb north of the *T'ung-yüan gate* (see above,—one of the northern gates). On the next day he made a halt in 海店 *Hai-tien*, which was 20 *li* distant from Yen-king. *Hai-tien* of that author is the same as 海淀 *Hai-tien* of our days.[11] It may be assumed from Wang Hui's notes (the Chinese author thinks), that the precincts (外郭) of the capital of the Kin were 75 *li* in circuit.[12]"

The preceding statements of the Chinese authors, drawn from ancient monuments, leave no doubt as to the position of ancient Peking since the 7th century; and it may be assumed that the town of the T'ang times, as well as the capitals of the Liao and the Kin, stood in about the same place, i. e. a little to the south-west of the present Tartar city; and their eastern wall was in the western part of the present Chinese city.

The rampart of an ancient city is found about 8 *li* to the south-west of the 彰儀門 *Chang-yi men* (gate), and at about the same distance from the 右安門 *Yu-an men*, which is the western gate in the southern wall of the Chinese city. Proceeding from this gate, about two *li* to the south one arrives at a small river running from west to east, through low-lying swampy meadows, forming here and there ponds. I shall speak more fully of it further on. Proceeding upward on the northern shore of this river for several *li*, one meets an ancient rampart, from 20 to 30 feet high, which stretches parallel with it. The rampart can be traced for more than seven *li*, and is generally well preserved. At the hamlet 鵝房營 *O-fang ying* the rampart turns to the north. Here was evidently the south-western corner of the ancient

---

10. The Mongol capital Khanbaligh was not yet built at that time. *K'ai-p'ing fu* is the same as *Shang-tu*, the summer residence of Coubilaï khan.
11. *Hai-tien* is now the name of a large village near the imperial summer gardens, north-west of Peking about 18 *li* distant in a straight direction from the south-western corner of the Tartar city.
12. This would explain the above-noticed discrepancy of the authors as to the circuit of the Kin capital (80 and 75 *li*).

city. Before reaching the stone road the rampart disappears. The corner is a very picturesque place. The rampart here is covered with beautiful white-barked pines (*pinus bungeana*) and tall *juniper* trees. A hundred paces to the west is a cemetery called 黑公墳地 *Hei-kung fen-ti*, surrounded by a wall, enclosing splendid groves of white-barked pines and juniper trees. About 2 *li* to the south-east the village of 柳材 *Liu-ts'un* is seen, which belongs to 豐臺 *Feng-t'ai*. The latter is a name, dating from the time of the Kin dynasty, and is now applied as a general designation to a number of villages renowned for their horticulture. According to the popular tradition, the rampart in question belonged in former times to the capital of the *Kin*, and this tradition is not in contradiction with the statements of Chinese authors regarding ancient *Chung-tu* (see above). There are also some traces of an ancient rampart several hundred paces north of the monastery of 白雲觀 *Po-yün kuan*. Here was probably the northern wall of the Kin city. As to the above-mentioned *O-fang ying*, people say that this name dates from the time of the Mongols, and that at this place water-fowl were kept for the emperor. *O-fang ying* may be translated "camp of the geese-keeper."

Coubilai khan, after having fixed his residence in Peking, built a new capital in 1267. Chinese literature devoted to the description of the Mongol capital is far from scarce. Some of the descriptions with many details, date from the Mongol times; others were compiled at the beginning of the Ming. The *Ji hia* quotes most of these authors, and brings together a great amount of material to elucidate the question of the position of ancient *Ta-tu*. But as we shall see, notwithstanding these detailed accounts, the antiquary meets with some difficulties in ascertaining the position of the ancient Mongol capital with respect to the present Peking, the ancient Chinese documents presenting some discrepancies.

The *Yüan shi*, chap. lviii, states:—In 1264 *Shi tsu* (Coubilai) established his residence at *Yen-king*; in 1267 he built the present city (present with respect to the Mongol time) to the *north-east* of the Kin capital, and fixed his residence in the new city, which in 1271 was called 大都 *Ta-tu*.

The above-mentioned work *Pei p'ing t'u king chi shu*, compiled at the end of the 14th century, says,—that the Mongol capital was built 3 *li* to the north (probably a misprint for north-east) of the city of the Kin.

Odoric, who visited Khanbaligh in the first half of the 14th century records (Yule's *Cathay*, vol. i, p. 127): "The Tartars took the old city, and then built another at a distance of *half-a-mile*, which they called *Taydo*."

Rashid-eddin, the able Persian historiographer, contemporary with Marco Polo, in his description of Khanbaligh states (D'Ohsson *Hist. des Mongols*, tom. ii, p. 633), "Comme la ville de *Tchoung dou* avait été ruinée par Tchinguiz khan, Coubilai voulait la restaurer; mais il aima mieux, pour la gloire de son nom, fonder une nouvelle ville près de l'ancienne, et il la nomma *Daï dou;* les deux sont contiguës."

The *Yuan shi* states further, that *Ta-tu* was 60 *li* in circumference. The 輟耕錄 *Ch'ue keng lu* (chap. xxi, fol. 1), a work published at the close of the Yüan dynasty (see Wylie's *Notes on Chinese Literature*, p. 159) gives the same number of *li* for the circuit of the capital, but explains, that *li* of 240 *pu* each are meant. (京城方六十里里二百四十步).[13] If this statement be correct, it would give only 40 common or geographical *li* for the circuit of the Mongol town.

Marco Polo in his description of Khanbaligh, gives it a compass of 42 miles,—6 miles for each side of the square.

The *Yüan shi*, as well as the *Chue keng lu*, and other works of the Yüan (see *Ji hia*, chap. xxxviii, fol. 1), agree in stating that the capital had eleven gates (Marco Polo and Odoric as is known, speak of twelve gates). They are enumerated in the following order.

Southern wall.

1. The gate direct south (mid.) was called 麗正門 *Li-cheng men*.
2. „ to the left (east) „ 文明門 *Wen-ming men*.
3. „ to the right (west) „ 順承門 *Shun-ch'eng men*.

Eastern wall.

4. The gate direct east (mid.) „ 崇仁門 *Ch'ung-jen men*
5. „ to the south-east „ 齊化門 *Ts'i-hua men*.
6. „ to the north-east „ 光熙門 *Kuang-hi men*.

Western wall.

7. The gate direct west (mid.) „ 和義門 *Ho-i men*.
8. „ to the south-west „ 平則門 *P'ing-tse men*.
9. „ to the north-west „ 肅清門 *Su-ts'ing men*.

---

13. The common Chinese 里 *li* has 360 步 *pu*, or 1·0 丈 *chang*, or 1800 尺 *ch'i* (feet). 1 *ch'i*=10 寸 *ts'un* (inches). 1 *li*=1,894 English feet or 575 mètres. Thus a *pu*=5 *ch'i*=5,26 English feet. It is an error into which all our authors of Chinese dictionaries have fallen, to translate 步 *pu* (5,26 English feet) simply by "pace," without any explanation. None of them have reflected, that a measure of more than 5 feet cannot be called a pace in our sense of the word. The Chinese consider the *pu* to contain two (of our) paces, and adduce for this view the argument, that a man has two legs and they require for a pace both legs to be moved. It seems, that in the middle ages the same view prevailed in Europe. At least according to the old Venice measures quoted in Yule's *M. Polo*, vol. ii, p. 472, one pace was=5 feet. Besides the common *li*, the Chinese have another *li*, used for measuring fields, which has only 240 *pu* or 1200 *ch'i*. This is the *li* spoken of in the *Ch'ue kang lu*. The length of the measures has not changed in China since the 11th century; at least this may be concluded from the ancient itineraries, in which distances are given.

Northern wall.

10. The gate to the north-west was called 健德門 *Ki'en-te men*.
11.   ,,   ,, north-east   ,, 安貞門 *An-chen men*.

The *Ji hia* (chap. xxxviii, fol. 2) quotes the *Yüan yi t'ung chi*, or "Great geography of the Mongol empire," and the 析津志 *Sin tsin chi* (early Ming time), both works stating, that at the time the Mongol capital was built, order was given to construct the southern wall at a distance of 30 *pu* south of the monastery of 慶壽寺 *King-shou sze*. This monastery had been founded about A. D. 1200, and the Mongols erected two beautiful *suburga* (towers) on it. It exists still with its suburgas, and is known under the name of 雙塔寺 *Shuang-ta sze* (the monastery of the double towers). About its position see my map. It is now distant 1⅓ *li* from the southern wall of the Tartar city. Perhaps there may be a mistake in the figures given, for the distance of the above-mentioned monastery from the southern wall of the Mongol capital; for other ancient Chinese statements can be quoted, pointing to the fact, that the Mongol southern wall was situated at the same place as the southern wall of the present Tartar city. F. i. the *Ta tu kung tien k'ao*, written in the early Ming times (see further on) states (*Ji hia*, chap. xxx, fol. 4), that *Li-cheng men* (the middle gate of the southern wall of Khanbaligh) was distant from the southern gate of the palace 920 *pu*; thus about the same distance as estimated now between *Ts'ien men* and the southern palace gate. I shall show further on, that the gates of the Mongol palace have been preserved in the surrounding wall of the prohibited city. In constructing my map of the ancient Mongol capital, from the native descriptions, it was necessary to decide in favour of one of these conflicting statements; and I have adopted the view that the southern wall was 920 *pu* distant from the southern gate of the palace. But I do not wish to impose my views on the reader. I have laid the several statements impartially before him, leaving him to draw his own conclusion. Further details about the site of ancient *Ta-tu* are found in the historical works of the Ming. The Mongols were overthrown and expelled from Peking by the Ming emperor *Hung-wu* in 1368. The detailed biography of Hung-wu, already quoted, states (*Ji hia*, chap. xxxviii, fol. 10, 11), "*Sü Ta* (a famed general of Hung-wu) ordered the officer *Hua Yün-lung* to measure the old city of the Yüan, and to build a new city, making the length from north to south equal to the length from east to west, which was 18,900 *ch'i* (feet).[14]

---

14. 大將軍徐達命指揮華雲龍經理故元都新築城垣南北取徑直東西長一千八百九十丈. I understand that each side of the square was 18,900 feet, i. e. =10.5 *li*, the circuit = 42 common *li*.

This somewhat obscure statement becomes more intelligible if we compare it with the following, found in the *Pei p'ing t'u king chi shu* (see above;—compare also *Ji hia*, chap. xxxviii, fol. 10): " Hung-wu, after having taken the Mongol capital, which was 60 *li* in circuit, found that it was too large, and ordered 5 *li* to be cut off at the northern part; and thus this part of the Mongol city, with the *Kuang-hi* and *Su-ts'ing* gates (the most northern ones of the eastern and western walls) was abandoned. The other nine gates remained the same. The new city was 40 *li* in circuit."[15]

It is not quite sure, whether the position of the wall of Peking remained at the same place after Hung-wu, or whether it was changed again by his successor *Yung-le*. I shall quote the statements of the Ming authors about it.

In the geographical section of the *Ming shi* it is stated: " In the year 1406, the emperor *Yung-le* decided to establish his residence in Peking. He ordered the imperial palace to be built, and the wall of the city to be repaired (修). In 1421 all was finished.[16] In 1437 the walls of Peking were faced with bricks. The city was then 45 *li* in circuit, and was pierced by nine gates. (The gates are all enumerated, and bear the same names as now.) In 1543 the southern suburbs were surrounded by a wall 28 *li* long (the present Chinese city)."

Finally the 工部志 *Kung pu chi* (Memoirs of the Board of public works of the Ming dynasty) gives the following accounts regarding the building of the Peking walls (*Ji hia*, chap. xxxviii, fol. 12): "When *Yung-le* decided to make Peking his residence he built the wall of the capital,[17] which was 40 *li* in circuit, and was pierced by nine gates as follows:—

" On the southern wall 麗正 *Li-cheng*, 文明 *Wen-ming* and 順承 *Shun-ch'eng* (These three names were preserved from the names of the southern gates of the Mongol city, but afterwards they were changed into the names they bear now. See the map).

" On the eastern wall 齊化 *Ts'i-hua* (name taken from the old city) and 東直 *Tung-chi* (new name).

---

15. The author has evidently forgotten to say, that the two northern gates (*Kien-te* and *An-chen*) of the Mongol city were transferred with the same names to the new northern wall. For otherwise his statement that nine gates remained the same cannot be made consistent with the shortening of the city. At another place in the same *T'ai tsu shi lu*, or "Biography of Hung-wu (see *Ji hia*, chap. iv, fol. 15)," it is stated that in 1369 the general *Sü Ta* changed the names of the Mongol northern gates *An-chen* and *Kien-te* into *An-ting* and *Te-sh'eng* (names still in use for the two northern gates of the modern capital).

16. The ambassador of *Shah Rokh* to the Chinese court, who arrived at Khanbaligh in December 1420, saw the walls in progress. The diarist of that embassy states (see *Indian Antiquary*, vol. ii, March, 1873, Bombay. "An embassy to Khatai"): "They arrived at the gate of Khanbaligh and obtained sight of a very large and magnificent city entirely built of stone; but as the outer walls were still being built, a hundred thousand scaffoldings concealed them."

17. 建築京城. These characters seem to denote that Yung-le built a new wall.

"On the western wall 平則 P'ing-tze (name taken from the old city) and 西直 Si-chi (new name).

"On the northern wall 安定 An-ting and 德勝 Te-sheng (both new names).

"In 1436 the names of the following gates were changed,—Li-cheng into 正陽 Cheng-yang, Wen-ming into 崇文 Ch'ung-wen, Shun-ch'eng into 宣武 Süan-wu, Tsi-hua into 朝陽 Ch'ao-yang and P'ing-tse into 阜城 Fou-ch'eng.[18]

"After the walls of Peking had been finished they measured as follows :—

The southern wall 12,959 ch'i, 3 ts'un, or (taking 1 li=1800 ch'i)= 7,2 li.
„ northern „ 22,324 „ 5 „ =12,4 „
„ eastern „ 17,869 „ 3 „ = 9,9 „
„ western „ 15,645 „ 2 „ = 8,7 „

Total 68,797 ch'i, or 38,2 li."

There is evidently a mistake in these figures, for the total gives not 40 li but only 38,2. It seems the figure for the southern wall is too small, for in reality it has about the same length as the northern one.

The site and appearance of the walls of the Peking Tartar city has not changed since the 15th century. It is therefore not without interest to compare these ancient Chinese measurements of the walls, with those made some months ago by the French astronomers, who observed the transit of Venus in Peking. Mr. *Fleuriais* and Mr. *Lapied* have had the kindness to communicate to me the results of their very carefully executed survey of the Peking walls.

The Tartar city is in circuit 23,55 kilomètres (or if we take the Chinese li=575 mètres)=41 li. Thus there is only 1 li difference with the Chinese measurements.

The southern wall measures 6,690 mètres, or 11,64 li.
„ northern „ 6,790 „ 11,81 „
„ eastern „ 5,330 „ 9,27 „
„ western „ 4,910 „ 8,54 „

Total. 41,26

Let me inquire now into the question, whether the above-quoted Chinese statements regarding the old Mongol capital can be made consistent with one of the ancient walls still seen in the neigh-

---

18. Since that, the names of the gates of Peking have not been changed. See the map (No. I) of modern Peking appended to this paper. There the popular names of the gates are also marked. Some of them, as for instance P'ing-tse men and Ts'i-hua men are as we have seen, ancient names of gates of Khanbaligh, and gates that stood probably at the same places as they do now.

borhood of Peking. One of these ancient records says, that the first emperor of the Ming cut off 5 *li* of the northern part of the Mongol city. Indeed, proceeding from one of the northern gates of the present Peking, 5 *li* to the north we meet a well-preserved ancient wall, which can be followed to an extent of more than seven English miles, and which joins the north-east and the north-west corners of the Tartar city. I have examined this ancient wall (土城 *t'u-ch'eng* "earthen wall" in Chinese) in its whole extent. It is an earthen wall from 20 to 30 feet high. Beginning at the moat near the north-eastern corner of Peking, it stretches 5 *li* in a northern direction and then turns to the west. At this corner seems to have been a large tower, judging from the round plateau found there. When the wall in its course to the west has reached the extension line of the western wall of Peking, it turns to the south. This corner had also a tower. At the water reservoir near the north-west corner of Peking, the ancient wall finishes. At distances of about 150 paces it sends outwards regular projections (bastions), the same as may be seen on the wall of modern Peking. Numerous paths and cart-ways leading to or from Peking, are cut through the ancient wall; but an attentive examination shows, that originally there were only four (or perhaps five) gates in the wall;—two to the north, opposite the *An-ting* and the *Te-sheng* gates; one to the east, and one (or perhaps two) to the west. For at these places the wall is pierced by broad passages. The two northern passages are known under the popular names of 東小關 *Tung-siao kuan* and 西小關 *Si-siao kuan* (eastern and western small barrier). At the Si-siao kuan, which is opposite the *Te-sheng* gate, and through which the road to *Kalgan* and *Kiakhta* passes, an ancient tower can be seen on the top of the wall. It is hollow but has no entrance.[19] The western wall had a gate about one English mile north of the north-west corner of present Peking. Here the great road from the Te-sheng gate to the summer palace now passes. Outside the gate we meet a circular wall as high as the rampart of the ancient city, close by but not in contact with it. It encloses a space of several hundred feet in diameter in which a temple (it seems of more recent date) is found. The circular wall in ancient times belonged probably to a fort. Not far from the north-western corner of the ancient rampart (*i. e.* south of the

---

19. An ancient tower of the same appearance is found about 14 *li* northward, on a hillock north-west of the village of 清河 *Ts'ing-ho* (also on the great highway to Kalgan); and similar towers are met frequently in the Peking plain, especially north of Peking. The Chinese call them 墩臺 *tun-t'ai*. They were used as beacon towers in ancient time. The Chinese beacon towers of the Ming times are well described by Persian travellers in the 15th century. See Dr. Zenker's translation of the *Khatai Nameh* in the *Zeitschr. f. d. Kunde des Morgenlandes* xv, band. These towers could only be ascended by rope ladders.

corner), we see on its top a small pavilion with a yellow roof, known to the people under the name of 皇亭 *Huang-t'ing* (imperial pavilion). In the pavilion is a large marble tablet, bearing on one side the inscription in large characters 薊門烟樹 *Ki-men yen-shu*, on the other side verses written by the emperor *Kien-lung* in the last century, and referring to the *Ki-men yen-shu* which was the name of a park in ancient times near this place. These four Chinese characters may be translated, "The somber trees near the gate of (ancient) *Ki*." There is a tradition, and this tradition existed long centuries ago, that at this spot was one of the gates of ancient *Ki* (see above). In the 水經注 *Shui king chu*, written in the 5th century of our era (at that time the city of Ki was still in existence), we find, that inside the city of *Ki* there is a hillock (邱), and therefore the city is also called 薊邱 *Ki k'iu* (see *Ji hia*, chap. cvii, fol. 4). In the *Ch'ang an k'o hua*, written at the end of the 16th century (see above), it is stated: "Outside of the *Te-sheng* gate we meet the *t'u-ch'eng kuan* (barrier of the earth wall). Tradition records, that here are the traces of ancient *Ki* or *Ki-k'iu*. There were in olden times, towers and palaces, but now (end of 16th century) all have disappeared; only one gate has been preserved, with two hillocks, one on each side. Contiguous to it is a park with beautiful vegetation and umbrageous trees. This park is one of the *eight beauties* [20] of the capital (*Ji hia*, chap. cvii, fol. 4)."

The park of *Ki-men* has been often celebrated by the poets of the Ming (*Ji hia*, chap. cvii, fol. 5); for instance, by 姚廣孝 *Yao Kuang-hiao*, who lived at the end of the 14th century (see Wylie's *Notes on Chinese Literature*, p. 148). In these poems of the Ming times, the *t'u-ch'eng* or ancient wall is also occasionally mentioned, but as to its origin no distinct indications are given. 程敏政 *Ch'eng Min-cheng*, who wrote in the middle of the 15th century (see Wylie, l.c. p. 29; and *Ming shi*, chap. cclxxxvi, Biographies), has left the following verses: "At the foot of the *t'u-ch'eng*, which is near the capital, the gates of an ancient monastery can be seen. The water roars.[21] All around are umbrageous

---

20. The 京都八景 *King tu pa king*, or "Eight beauties of the Capital," are enumerated in ancient descriptions of Peking as follows. 1. The above-mentioned *Ki-men yen-shu*; 2. The 瓊華島 *K'iung-hua tao*, an island in the lake near the imperial palace. I shall speak of it further on; 3. The 西苑 *Si yüan*, or "Imperial gardens," near the same lake; 4. The 西山 *Si shan* or "Western hills;" 5. The hill 玉泉山 *Yü-ts'üan shan*; 6. The bridge 盧溝橋 *Lu-kou k'iao*; 7. The defile 居庸 *Kü-yung* (already mentioned); 8. The 黃金台 *Huang-kin t'ai*, a tower built, as tradition records, by *Chao wang*, prince of *Yen*, several thousand years ago. According to the *Ch'ang an k'o hua*, chap. i, fol. 7, it was situated east of Peking; in the *Ch'un ming*, chap. xv, fol. i, it is stated, that this denomination of the eight beauties dates from the time of the Kin dynasty.

21. The moat of the ancient rampart exists still at its northern part, and near the above mentioned barrier *Si-siao kuan*, a marble bridge spans it.

trees and numerous people walk about. Here is the gate of ancient *Ki*. From the time of the *Kin* and the *Yüan*, only one old tower has been left behind." Whether the author speaks of the above-mentioned beacon tower, or of a tower which at his time may still have existed near the north-western corner of the ancient rampart, I am not prepared to say. The earliest author of the Ming who speaks of the *Ki-men yen-shu* park is 金 幼 孜 *Kin Yu-tze*, who lived at the end of the 14th century. See his verses quoted in the *Ch'ang an k'o hua*, chap. i, fol. 4.

The park celebrated in the ancient poems does not exist at the present time. There are some groups of trees scattered over the fields near the pavilion of Kien-lung, but they do not inspire idyllic thoughts. The hillock alluded to in ancient writings, seems to have been comprised in the rampart itself. Kien-lung's pavilion stands on the rampart, which at this place is about ten feet higher than the rest. Beside the pavilion is a passage through the wall, by which one of the roads leads to the summer palace.

I have not been able to find in works written during the Ming, any more precise indications than the above quoted, regarding the origin of the ancient rampart north of Peking; and the question whether it is the Mongol wall, or whether it belonged to ancient *Ki* cannot be decided from old Chinese documents. Some of the modern Chinese writers incline to the first view; others consider the wall as belonging to ancient Ki. The emperor Kien-lung it seems subscribed to the latter opinion. But the views of the Chinese authors of the present dynasty, as regards this wall, are of no value, being entirely arbitrary. As we can judge only from Chinese documents, and as these documents are contradictory, the question is not easy to settle. After having carefully compared most of the accounts given in the *Ji hia* and other books regarding the position of Peking in the Mongol time, I incline to the following view.

It is almost certain, as we have seen, that the north-eastern corner of the Kin capital was somewhere near the south-western corner of the present Tartar city. The *Yüan shi* states that the new capital of the Mongols was built north-east of the ancient one. An author of the 14th century gives the distance between the new and the old city equal to 3 *li;* Odoric says half a mile. *Hung-wu*, the first Ming emperor is stated to have cut off 5 *li* of the northern part of the Mongol capital. He built the northern wall of Peking at the same place where it now stands.

It seems that the emperor Yung-le built the southern, the eastern and the western walls of the present Peking, on the ancient ramparts of Khanbaligh; and this supposition would be in accordance with a statement found in the *Ch'ang an k'o hua*, chap. i, fol. 3, 都城周廻四十里並元舊基 *i. e.* "The capital (of the Ming) is 40 *li* in circuit; the wall of it was built on the ancient wall of the Yüan."

As to the ancient rampart north of Peking, I am disposed to sustain the view of Col. Yule, that it is the wall of Khanbaligh, notwithstanding the fact, that no Chinese author of the Ming seems to mention it as a wall of the Mongol capital. They mention it only in connection with *Ki*. The city of Ki may have been at the same place where now the wall passes; but if it be taken into consideration that this rampart is well preserved, and that it must have been the wall of a large city (of which the remains evidently surrounded only a part, the other part being comprised in the modern Tartar city), we cannot assign to it so remote an origin, and cannot attribute it to Ki, which hardly was a large city.

Thus I have traced according to my judgment,—which however is partly in contradiction with the above-quoted ancient Chinese records,—the outlines of Khanbaligh, which, if my view be correct, would have measured about 50 common *li* in circuit (13 *li* and more from north to south, 11.64 from east to west). Marco Polo states that Khanbaligh was a square, each side measuring 6 miles. I may quote yet another statement of the great traveller,—generally so trusty in his reports, regarding Khanbaligh,—which is in accordance with the accounts of contemporary Chinese authors, and which supports my view. Marco Polo states (l. c. vol. i, p. 332), "Moreover, in the middle of the city [Khanbaligh] there is a great clock—that is to say, a bell—which is struck at night, etc." The traveller speaks of the bell-tower (鐘樓 *chung-lou*). The *Yüan yi t'ung chi*, or "Geography of the Mongol empire (quoted in the *Ji hia*, chap. xxxviii, fol. 1)" records 至元九年建鐘鼓樓於城中, *i. e.* "In the year 1272, the bell-tower and the drum-tower were built *in the middle* of the capital." A bell-tower (*chung-lou*) and a drum-tower (*ku-lou*) exist still in Peking, in the northern part of the Tartar city (see the map). The *ku-lou* is the same as that built in the 13th century, but the bell-tower dates only from the last century. The bell-tower of the Yüan was a little to the east of the drum-tower, where now the temple *Wan-ning sze* stands *(Ji hia*, chap. liv, fol. 11, 12). This temple is nearly in the middle of the position I assign to Khanbaligh.

There is an ancient rampart east of Peking, stretching from south to north. It begins at the northren border of the *T'ung-chou* canal, about one English mile east of the *T'ung-pien* gate, and can be pursued with certainty in its course to the north, parallel with the eastern wall of Peking, as far as to the stone road, leading from the *T'si-hua* gate to *T'ung-chou*. The present foreign race-ground lies near this rampart, which seems to be of more ancient date than the northern rampart above mentioned. It is lower than the first and in a more demolished state; at some places it has entirely disappeared. No connection can be made out between it and the northern rampart. A small river, probably the ancient moat, runs along the eastern side of this wall, and the stone road crosses the river on a marble bridge. Mr. Edkins (l. c. p. 385) identifies this eastern ancient wall also with the wall of the Mongol city; but it seems to me, there is no reason for this supposition. It is strange, that the *Ji hia* does not mention at all this eastern ancient wall. If one asks the people about it he will hear, that it dates from the time of the empress 蕭 *Siao* of the *Liao* dynasty.[22] But as we have seen, the Liao capital was to the south-west of the present Peking, and the authors of the Ming mention this empress often in connection with ancient vestiges south-west of the capital.[32]

The present Tartar city, or the northern city of Peking, 內城 *Nei-ch'eng*, which as I have suggested, occupies for the greater part, the space comprised in former times in Khanbaligh, appears on the map to be composed of three concentric squares. The outermost is the wall of the Tartar city, which is as we have seen 41 *li* in circuit. The middle square is the 皇城 *Huang-ch'eng* or "Imperial city," the surrounding wall of which measures 18 *li*, and is pierced by four principal gates, corresponding to the four cardinal points of the compass. The southern wall has, besides the large gate, two smaller lateral gates. The innermost of the walled squares is the 紫禁城 *Tze-kin-ch'eng* (Red prohibited city) containing the palace. The surrounding wall measures 6.3 *li* (3.6 kilomètres), and is encompassed by a broad and deep moat. But this is not the only prohibited ground in the imperial city. There is another walled square north of the *Tze-kin-ch'eng* in which the hill 景山 *King shan* lies. This is also inaccessible to the public, as well as the imperial gardens, which border on the beautiful lake, stretching from north to south in the imperial city, and which are also protected by walls. The remaining part of

---

22. The 都城形勢考 *Tu ch'eng hing shi k'ao*, a short historical description of Peking, published in the present century, is the only Chinese work which records this popular tradition. The author however is of opinion, that the eastern ancient rampart belonged to the outer wall of the *Liao* or *Kin* capital, also a completely arbitrary statement.
23. The name of this valiant empress, who commanded the army in person in the beginning of the 11th century, is even now very popular in Peking. There is a Chinese romance 十二寡婦西征, treating of her exploits. In a battle fought with the army of the *Sung*, near the village of *Kuan-shi*, 50 *li* north-west of Peking, six sons of the empress perished. At the top of the hill 望兒山 *Wang-rh shan*, which is the most eastern spur of the mountains projecting into the plain, she built a temple commemorative of the battle, from which the battle-field could be seen. The ruins of this temple still exist.

the imperial city, to the west and east of the imperial grounds, is left to the people. But as to the communication between the eastern and western parts of the city, there is only one road left for the public, which turns round the King shan to the north and crosses the lake by a handsome marble bridge. The Chinese on foot are allowed to pass between the King shan and the imperial palace square, when they wear an official hat. This right is as yet denied to foreigners in European costume. The French missionaries however, who are dressed *à la Chinoise*, are not prevented from passing so near to the imperial palace.

The 景山 *King shan*, called also 煤山 *Mei shan* (Coal mount) in the popular language, is a lovely hill nearly 200 feet high, covered with splendid trees, for the most part white-barked pines (Pinus Bungeana), *Juniperus Chinensis*, and *Pinus Massoniana*. It has several prominences crowned with beautiful pavilions and temples. The surrounding wall is about 1¾ *kilomètre* in circuit. The hill occupies only the southern part of the enclosure. According to the measurements of the French astronomers, the King shan is nearly in the centre of the Tartar city.

The traveller, who visits the beauties of the capital, generally does not fail to repair to the handsome marble bridge which crosses the above-mentioned lake. It is the only point from which he is allowed to admire the picturesque view of the imperial gardens (西苑 *Si yüan*) bordering on the lake. The bridge, known under the Chinese name 金鼇玉蝀 *Kin-ao yü-tung*, has ten arches and is 220 (European) paces long. Near the eastern end of the bridge the visitor sees a circular wall, which is called 圓城 *yüan ch'eng* (round wall). It is about 350 paces in circuit. Within it is an imperial building 承光殿 *Ch'eng-kuang tien*, dating from the Mongol time. From this circular enclosure, another long and beautifully executed marble bridge leads northward, to a charming hill, covered with shady trees, and capped by a magnificent white *suburga*.[24] There are many other buildings on this hill. At the present day it forms a peninsula, but in ancient times it was an island in the lake. The peninsula however is still separated from the shore by a river. It is called 白塔山 *Pai-t'a shan* (Hill of the white suburga), but is known also under its ancient name 瓊華島 *K'iung-hua tao*. The lake, which in summer is covered with splendid lotus flowers, and frequented by herons and other marsh and water fowls, bears the name 太液池 *T'ai-yi ch'i*, a name by which it was known as early as the 12th century, when the waters from the western hills were first led to this place.

I shall not enter into more particulars regarding the modern

---

24. It dates A. D. 1651. These *suburga*, frequently seen in Peking and its environs, have all the shape of a bellied decanter.

palace grounds, for they can be found in many books referring to Peking. My intention is rather to compare the accounts M. Polo and other mediæval travellers give of the same places, with the statements of Chinese authors contemporary with these travellers, or near to their times.

In the *Ji hia*, three chapters (xxx-xxxii) are devoted to the description of the palaces and the imperial grounds at the time of the Mongols. In the introduction to these accounts it is stated, that they have been drawn from several works of the Mongol dynasty, or of the early Ming time, preserved in the 永樂大典 *Yung le ta tien*, the gigantic cyclopædia completed in 1407, containing nearly 23,000 books (see Wylie's *Notes on Chinese Literature*, p. 149). The *Ji hia* quotes the 禁扁 *Kin pien* (List of the palaces of the Yüan), and the 元宮室製 *Yüan kung shi chi*; but states, that the most detailed description of the Mongol palaces are found in the 昭儉錄 *Chao kien lu* and the 輟耕錄 *Ch'ue keng lu*. The latter work, as I have stated, was published towards the end of the Mongol dynasty. The author of this work, who lived in *Che-kiang*, speaks it seems not as an eye-witness; but had drawn his information, as he says, from a Mongol governor in Che-kiang, who had been governor in the capital in former times. Another ancient description of the Mongol palaces exists under the name of 故宮遺錄 *Ku kung i lu*, compiled during the reign of the first Ming emperor (see Wylie, *N. on C. L.* p. 48). The *Ji hia* quotes also the 大都宮殿考 *Ta tu kung tien k'ao* published in the time of the Ming.

The description of the imperial palaces at different times, as found in the *Ji hia*, leave no doubt that the palace of the Mongols as well as of the Ming occupied about the same space as the palace of the present dynasty now occupies. This has already been presumed by Col. Yule (see his M. Polo vol. i, p. 331). Even some of the names of the gates in the palace enclosure of the Mongol khans have been preserved in the gate-names of the modern prohibited city (see further on).

Before entering into details, I may be allowed to give explanations of some terms occurring in the Chinese descriptions of the palaces.

The palace buildings occupied by the emperor bear the general name 大內 *Ta-nei* (Great interior). 宮 *Kung* is a general term comprising a number of palace buildings and their appurtenances. The single buildings are differently termed according to their construction and destination. 殿 *Tien* is a first-rank palace building, generally a throne-hall and always of one story. 閣 *Ko* is a second-rank palace building, often of two stories. 堂 *T'ang* is a hall; 亭 *T'ing*, a pavilion; 樓 *Lou*, a large storied tower. A good drawing of a *lou* is found in Yule's M. Polo, vol. i, p. 335. According to these categories the palace buildings of the Mongols are enumerated in the *Kin pien* (*Ji hia*, chap. xxx, fol. 1,2). The same work states, that there were three 宮 *kung* in the Mongol capital; one of them east of the lake, occupied by the emperor; two west of the lake and occupied as other Chinese authors state, by Coubilaï khan's son and by some of the empresses.

M. Polo states (l. c. vol. i, pp. 324, 325):—"[The great palace of the Kaan] is enclosed all round by a great wall forming a square, each side of which is a mile (2.77 Chin. *li* [25]) in length; that is to say, the whole compass thereof is *four* miles (about 11 *li*)"...... Inside of this wall there is a second, enclosing a space that is somewhat greater in length than in breadth... In the middle of the second enclosure is the Lord's Great Palace."

There are however some discrepancies in the different texts of Marco Polo, as to the number and the circuit of the palace enclosures (l. c. vol. i, p. 328, note 4). Ramusio's version "makes the inner enclosure a mile (2.77 *li*) square; outside of this it puts another of *six* miles (16.6 *li*) square, and at a mile interval, a third of *eight* miles (22 *li*) square." Pauthier's text regarding this question is unintelligible.

Before giving the detailed description of the Mongol palace according to the Chinese authors, I may first observe, that in the ancient Chinese works three concentric enclosures are mentioned in connection with the palace. The innermost enclosed the 大內 *Ta-nei*, the middle enclosure, called 宮城 *Kung-ch'eng* or 皇城 *Huang-ch'eng*, answering to the wall surrounding the present prohibited city, and was about 6 *li* in circuit. Besides this there was an outer wall (a rampart apparently) 20 *li* in circuit, answering to the wall of the present imperial city (which now has 18 *li* in circuit).

In the great biography of the first Ming emperor (*T'ai tsu shi lu*;— see *Ji hia*, chap. xxxviii, fol. 11), it is stated, that the 皇城 *Huang-ch'eng*[26] of the Yüan was measured by imperial order, and found to be 12,600 *ch'i* (or Chin. feet), or 7 *li* in circuit. The *Ch'ue keng lu*, as we shall see further on, makes the wall of the Mongol palace=10,950 *ch'i*, or 6 *li* in circuit.

The author of the *Ch'ue keng lu* devotes two long articles to the description of the palace of the Mongols and the adjacent palace grounds. One is entitled 宮闕制度 *Kung küe chi tu*, "Topography of the palace" (chap. xxi). The other is found in the first chapter under the title 萬歲山 *Wan sui shan*, and describes a hill situated to the north-west

---

25. According to the old Venice measures (Yule's M. Polo, vol. ii, p. 472), *one* mile=5000 feet. Thus M. Polo's mile could be approximately estimated=2.77 Chinese *li*.

26. I must observe, that the term *Huang-ch'eng*, now applied to the imperial city, which is 18 *li* in circuit, and the wall of which was first built under the Ming, must not be confounded with what the biography of the first Ming emperor calls *Huang-ch'eng*; for this was the enclosure of the palace, answering to the present prohibited city. This results from the Chinese statements regarding the circuit of the Mongol *Huang-ch'eng*. At the present day the circuit of the prohibited city is estimated by the Chinese=11,320 *ch'i*=6.3 *li*. I may further observe that 城 *ch'eng* in Chinese means *city* as well as *wall*.

of the palace. I shall give the translation of the greater part of these accounts, to enable the reader to compare them with M. Polo's statements. The *Ku kung i lu* gives also a detailed description of the palace and the pleasure-grounds (*Ji hia*, chap. xxxii, fol. 24-31), which is generally in accordance with the *Ch'ue keng lu*.

After having given the figures for the circuit of the Mongol capital, and the names of the eleven gates, as above stated, the *Ch'ue keng lu* continues as follows:—

"The imperial palace (大內) has to the south in its neighborhood the *Li-cheng* gate.[27] The principal halls of the palace are the 大明殿 *Ta-ming tien* and the 延春閣 *Yen-ch'un ko*.

"The wall surrounding the palace (宮城)[28] is 9 *li* 30 *pu* in circuit. It measures from east to west 480 *pu*, and from north to south 615 *pu*.[29] It is constructed of bricks, and is 35 *ch'i* in height.[30] The construction was begun in A. D. 1271, on the 17th of the 8th month, between three and five o'clock in the afternoon, and finished next year on the 15th of the 3rd month. The wall is pierced by six gates (門 *men*) of which three are on its southern face.

"The 崇天門 *Ch'ung-tien men* is in the middle of the southern wall. This gate comprises twelve *kien*[31] and has five gateways. It measures 187 *ch'i* from east to west, 55 in depth, and 85 in height. To the left and right respectively of the gate, is a tower (樓 *lou*). (I omit the particulars regarding these towers.) Near the southern face of the wall are barracks for the life-guards.[32]

"The gate east of Ch'ung-t'ien men is called 星拱門 *Sing-kung men*. It comprises three *kien* and has one gateway. From east to west is 55 *ch'i*; depth, 45; height, 50. The gate west of Ch'ung-t'ien men is called 雲從門 *Yün-tsung men*, and the measures are the same as the Sing-kung men.

"The gate in the eastern wall is called 東華門 *Tung-hua men*;

---

27. This gate was in the middle of the southern wall of the Mongol capital;—see above.
28. Rashid-eddin states (*D'Ohsson*, l. c. tom. ii, p. 634), that Coubilaï built in the middle of the capital, a vast palace, which was called *Carschi*. Klaproth explains (*Nouveau Journal Asiatique*, tom. xi), that *carschi* in Mongol is the same as 殿 *tien* (hall) in Chinese. But he is wrong. Now at least, *carshi* in Mongol means an enclosure; and in this case seems to answer to the Chinese 宮城 *Kung-ch'eng*.
29. This makes 1290 *pu* for the circuit; and as the measures in the *Ch'ue keng lu* are not estimated in common *li*, but in *li* of 240 *pu* (comp. note 13), 1290 *pu* = 9 *li* 30 *pu*.
30. M. Polo says the wall surrounding the palace is "very thick, and a good ten paces in height, white-washed and loop-holed all round."
31. 間 *kien* properly means a division of a room made by the framework, but it may be taken as a unit for measuring rooms. However, the extent of the *kien* varies according to the elevation of the building.
32. M. Polo states (l. c. vol. i, p. 325): "Towards the south [of the palace] there is a vacant space which the Barons and the soldiers are constantly traversing."

that in the western wall, 西華門 *Si-hua men*.[33] As to their measures, they are the same on both; seven *kien*, three gateways, etc.

"The gate on the northern face of the wall is called 厚載門 *Hou-tsai men*; five *kien*, one gateway, etc.

"In each of the four corners of the *Kung-ch'eng*, there is a tower (*lou*). The roofs have glazed tiles.

"Opposite the *Ch'ung-t'ien men*, there is a *marble bridge* with twining dragons sculptured on it. It has three arches and three passages, the middle one being especially appropriated to the emperor.[34]

"South of the gate *Sing-kung men* (*i. e.* outside the Kung-ch'eng) there is a pavilion, where the emperor sometimes takes breakfast (御膳亭). East of this pavilion is the hall 拱辰堂 *Kung-ch'en t'ang*, in which the officers (going to the court) use to assemble. To the east of the tower, which is in the south-eastern corner of the Kung-ch'eng, and a little to the north is the storehouse for raw productions (生料庫), and to the east of the storehouse is the yard for fuel (柴場). Between the two walls[35] in the north-eastern corner is a paddock for sheep (羊圈). At the south-western corner, outside the 南紅門 *Nan-hung men*[36] is the residence of the 留守司 *Liu-shou-sze*.[37] To the south of the gate *Si-hua men* is the 儀鸞局 (a storehouse for carts, sedan chairs, etc.); to the west of it is the 鷹房, the place where the falcons are kept. To the north of the *Hou-tsai* gate is the imperial garden (御苑).[38]

"The outer rampart (外周垣) surrounding the palace ground[39]

---

33. The names *Tung-hua men* and *Si-hua men* have been preserved in the names of the eastern and western gates of the present prohibited city. These gates have three gateways, as in the Mongol time.
34. The position of this bridge is more explicitly given in the *Ku kung i lu* (*Ji hia*, chap. xxix, fol. 24). There it is stated: "To the north of the *Li-cheng* gate (answering the present 前門 *Ts'ien men*) is the gallery 千步廊 *Ts'ien-pu lang* (a gallery of this name bordering on both sides the approach to the palace still exists. See the map, and comp. *Ji hia*, chap. ix, fol. 3.) At a distance of about 700 *pu* (from the *Li-cheng* gate) the gate 靈星門 *Ling-sing men* had been erected; and here passes a rampart (蕭牆 *siao ts'iang*), which is 20 *li* in circuit, and bears the popular name 紅門闌馬牆 *Hung men lan ma ts'iang*. 20 *pu* inside (*i. e.* to the north of the rampart) is a river. A marble bridge with three passages spans it. The *Ch'ung-t'ien men* is 200 *pu* distant from this bridge. It seems to me, that the river here spoken of is the 金水 *Kin shui*, which comes out from the lake. Now it passes south of the 天安門 *T'ien-an men*, where five marble bridges, called 金水橋 *Kin-shui k'iao* span it. See map II.
35. 夾垣 means between two walls. Perhaps the author intends between the Kung-ch'eng and the outer wall spoken of in note 34.
36. This gate was in the outer wall it seems.
37. *Liu-shou-sze* is a governor in the capital. When the emperor left, the *Liu-shou-sze* supplied his place.
38. Where now the hill *King shan* stands.
39. By the outer rampart the Chinese author understands it seems, the rampart mentioned in note 35, which was 20 *li* in circuit.

has fifteen red gates;[40] the inner garden (內苑), five red gates; the imperial garden, four red gates. These gardens are all between the two walls."[41]

After having spoken of the Kung-ch'eng and its six gates, and having mentioned some imperial buildings and storehouses between the Kung-ch'eng and the outer wall, the author of the *Ch'ue keng lu* proceeds to the description of the *Ta-nei* (imperial palace), situated inside the Kung-ch'eng, and enumerates the gates leading to the *Ta-nei* or connecting the palace yards. It seems that the inner enclosure surrounding the palace was a gallery, through which the gates passed. In my translation of these accounts regarding the Mongol palace I have occasionally been obliged to omit some particulars, being unintelligible even for the Chinese. The *Ch'ue keng lu* continues as follows:—

"The gate 大明門 *Ta-ming men* is situated towards the interior, with respect to the *Ch'ung-t'ien men* (*i. e.* north of it). It is the principal (southern) gate leading to the *Ta-ming tien* (see below). It comprises seven *kien* and has three gateways. From east to west = 120 *ch'i*; in depth, 44. It has double eaves.[42]

"The gate to the east of Ta-ming men is called 日精門 *Ji-tsing men*; that to the west, 月華門 *Yüe-hua men*. Both are of one gateway.[43]

"The 大明殿 *Ta-ming tien* (Hall of great brightness) is the first of the halls in the palace. Here the emperor gives solemn audiences on occasion of the accession to the throne, at new year, and on his birthday. This building comprises eleven *kien*, measures 200 *ch'i* from east to west, 120 *ch'i* in depth, and 90 in height. The pillared verandah (柱廊) comprises seven *kien*, is 240 *ch'i* long, 44 broad, and 50 in height. (Besides this) the building has five *kien* of dwelling rooms

---

40. 紅門 *Hung men*, "red gates." This seems to be a general term for small gates in the ramparts surrounding parks, etc. The rampart now surrounding the park south of Peking, known under the name of 南海子 *Nan-hai-tze*, has nine gates, and five of them are called red gates (a northern, southern, etc., red gate).
41. M. Polo states (l. c. vol. i, p. 326): "Between the two walls of the enclosure which I have described, there are fine Parks and beautiful trees, etc." But as has been stated, some confusion has crept into the texts of M. P. as to the number and position assigned to the enclosures.
42. 重簷 "Double eaves." See the drawing of a gate of Peking in Yule's M. Polo, vol. i, p. 335.
43. The last-mentioned three gates (the middle one with three gateways) seem to have been opposite the three gates in the southern wall of the Kung-cheng. M. Polo speaks of five gates, which the palace wall had "on its southern face, the middle one being the great gate which is never opened on any occasion except when the Great Kaan himself goes forth or enters. Close on either side of this great gate is a smaller one by which all other people pass; and then towards each angle is another great gate, also open to people in general; so that on that side there are five gates in all. Inside of this wall there is a second,.........(which) also hath five gates on the southern face, corresponding to those in the outer wall......In the middle of the second enclosure is the Lord's Great Palace." It seems Polo took the three gateways in the middle gate for three gates, and thus speaks of five gates instead of three in the southern wall.

(寢室), and six *kien* of other rooms, contiguous to the eastern and western ends of the hall.[44]

"To the north the Ta-ming tien is in connection with another building called 香閣 Hiang-ko (Fragrant hall. This seems to be a general term for buildings adjoining halls.), and comprising three *kien*. It measures 140 *ch'i* from east to west, 50 in depth, and 70 in height. It has been constructed of beautifully-wrought stones of different colours. The pillars are of a red colour and richly adorned with gold and twining dragons. Thick carpets are spread out on the floor. There is a divan for the emperor (御榻) covered with gold brocade, and adorned with precious stones. There are also seats for the empresses, the princes, the officers, and the 怯薛 *k'ie-sie*.[45] At festive entertainments the seats are arranged to the right and left of the emperor, according to the ranks (重列).[46]

"In the front there has been put up a *clepsydra* with a lantern (燈漏). By means of machinery put in motion by water, at fixed times a little man comes forward exhibiting a tablet, which announces the hours.[47]

"There is further a *large jar* made of wood and *varnished*,[48] the inside lined with silver (木質銀裹漆甕一). A dragon in golden clouds twines around the jar, which is 17 feet in height and holds more than 50 piculs (石) of wine. There is also a jar of jade (玉甕)."[49]

44. The *Ta-ming tien* is without doubt what M. Polo calls "the Lord's Great Palace,—the greatest Palace that ever was." He states, that it "hath no upper story;" and indeed, as I explained above, the palace buildings which the Chinese call *tien*, are always of one story. Polo speaks also of a "very fine pillared balustrade" (the *chu lang* of the Chinese author). M. Polo states that the basement of the great palace "is raised some ten palms above the surrounding soil." We find in the *Ku kung i lu* (*Ji hia*, chap. xxxii, fol. 24): "The basement of the Ta-ming tien (大明殿基) is raised about 10 *ch'i* above the soil." There can also be no doubt, that the Ta-ming tien stood at about the same place, where now the 太和殿 *T'ai-ho tien*, the principal hall of the palace is situated. See maps II and III.
45. The four *k'ie-sie* repeatedly spoken of in the Yüan shi, commanding the khan's life-guards. They are mentioned also by Rashid-eddin. Odoric calls them "Cuthe (Zuche);" the four barons "keeping watch and ward over the chariot" in which the Caan travelled (Yule's *Cathay*, vol. i, p. 135).
46. M. Polo in describing the high feasts of the great Kaan reads as follows: (l. c. vol. i. p. 338): "And when the Great Kaan sits at table on any great court occasion, it is in this fashion. His table is elevated a good deal above the others, and he sits at the north end of the hall, looking towards the south, with his chief wife beside him on the left. On his right sit his sons and his nephews, and other kinsmen of the Blood Imperial, but lower, so that their heads are on a level with the Emperor's feet. And then the other Barons sit at other tables lower still: so also with the women;.........each (sits) in the place assigned by the Lord's orders."
47. A more detailed description of this clepsydra in the hall of the emperor is given in the *Yüan shi* (comp. *Ji hia*, chap. xxx, fol. 15). There it is said amongst other things that it was made of gold and richly hung with pearls.
48. Perhaps this statement may serve to explain M. Polo's "*verniques*" or "*vaselle vernicate d'oro*," big enough to hold drink for eight or ten persons (l. c. vol. i, p. 339).
49. Another large jar of jade is mentioned in one of the other halls (see note 63 and the corresponding text). I am not able to say, whether one of these jars may be identified with the jar seen by Odoric in the Great Khan's palace, and described by him in the following

After this the *Ch'ue keng lu* describes the musical instruments found in the hall. I omit the details; but I shall mention a statement regarding the musical instruments at the Mongol court, from the same work found in chapter v, under the head of 興隆笙 *Hing-lung sheng;* for it furnishes evidence of the authenticity of Odoric's narrative. The 笙 *sheng* is a certain wind instrument composed of reeds inserted in a gourd bulb, with a bent blow-tube; *hing-lung* means "prosperous." The *Ch'ue keng lu* states that in the hall *Ta-ming tien* there is a *hing-lung sheng.* When, on the occasion of a great entertainment given by the emperor, this instrument begins to play, the whole orchestra chimes in. The instrument is in connection, by means of a tube, with *two peacocks* sitting on a cross-bar; and when it plays, the mechanism causes the peacocks to dance (笙首爲二孔雀笙鳴機動則應而舞).

Odoric's narrative reads as follows:—"In the hall of the palace also are many peacocks of gold. And when any of the Tartars wish to amuse their lord, then they go one after the other and clap their hands; upon which the peacocks flap their wings, and make as if they would dance. Now this must be done either by diabolic art, or by some engine underground." M. Polo, in describing the Great Kaan's table at his high feasts (*l. c.* vol. i, p. 340), mentions also the musical instruments. He says:—"And when the Emperor is going to drink, all the musical instruments, of which he has vast store of every kind, begin to play."

The *Ch'ue keng lu* continues the description of the halls in the palace as follows:—"There is also a table for wine with figures carved on it (雕象酒桌) 8 *ch'i* long, and 7 *ch'i* 2 *ts'un* broad.[50] ...... In winter time the walls of the rooms in the principal hall (大殿) are hung with skins of *yellow cats* (黃猫皮), whilst on the floor *black sable* skins (黑貂) are spread. But in the *Hiang-ko* (see above) the walls are hung with *ermine* skins (銀鼠皮), and the alcoves (煖帳) with sable skins.[51]

---

terms (Yule's *Cathay,* vol. i, p. 130): "In the midst of the palace is a certain great jar, more than two paces in height, entirely formed of a certain precious stone called *Merdacas.* ......It is all hooped round with gold, and in every corner thereof is a dragon represented as in act to strike most fiercely. And this jar hath also fringes of network of great pearls hanging therefrom.......Into this vessel drink is conveyed by certain conduits from the court of the palace." As to the word "merdacas," it has no meaning in modern Mongol; but "jade" is *kash* in Mongol.

50. Compare the following passage in M. Polo's account (*l.c.* vol. i, pp. 338,339): "In a certain part of the hall near where the Great Kaan holds his table, there [is set a large and very beautiful piece of workmanship in the form of a square coffer, or buffet, about three paces each way, exquisitely wrought with figures of animals, finely carved and gilt. The middle is hollow, and in it] stands a great vessel of pure gold, holding as much as an ordinary butt; and at each corner of the great vessel is one of smaller size [of the capacity of a firkin], and from the former the wine or beverage, flavoured with fine and costly spices is drawn off into the latter."

51. M. Polo does not mention the skins used in the palace at Cambaluc, but in describing the

"The roof of the palace is made of glazed tiles; the eaves and the ridges of the roofs are adorned (probably with little stone animals,— as is done now)."

After the principal edifice of the palace, the *Ta-ming tien*, the largest of all, the Chinese author describes the other halls of the *Ta-nei*. I omit, in my translation, the measures given in the Chinese text, for they are of little interest.

"The 文思殿 *Wen-sze tien* (which was a small building) is situated to the east of the dwelling-rooms of the Ta-ming tien.

"The 紫檀殿 *Tze-t'an tien*, is to the west of the Ta-ming tien. This hall is constructed entirely of *Tze-t'an*.[52]

"The 寶雲殿 *Pao-yün tien* is situated behind (*i. e.* to the north of) the dwelling-rooms of the Ta-ming tien. (I omit the details.)

"The gate 鳳儀門 *Feng-i men* is in the middle of the eastern side-gallery (在東廡中); it has one gateway. Outside this gate are the lodgings for the cooks (庖人之室), and rather more to the south, the lodgings for the wine-keepers (酒人之室).

"The gate 麟瑞門 *Lin-jui men* is in the middle of the western side-gallery; and has also one gateway. Outside this gate is the store-house for the palace (內藏庫); which has twenty rooms, each of them comprising seven *kien*.

"A *bell-tower* (鐘樓) stands south of the *Feng-i men*; and a *drum-tower* (鼓樓) south of the *Lin-jui men*. Both are 75 *ch'i* in height.

"The gate 嘉慶門 *Kia-k'ing men* is situated in the back (*i. e.* northern) gallery (在後廡), to the east of the *Pao-yün tien* (the *Kin pien* says to the north-east of it).

"The gate 景福門 *King-fu men* is situated in the northern gallery, to the west of the *Pao-yün tien* (the *Kin pien* says to the north-west of it). Both gates are of one gateway.

"The surrounding gallery (周廡) comprises a hundred and twenty *kien*, and is 35 *ch'i* in height. In the four corners are towers (*lou*) each of four *kien*; their roofs have double eaves. The pillars in the gallery are all painted red; the walls are beautifully wrought; the roof is made of glazed tiles; the eaves and the ridges are adorned.[53]

---

great travelling tents of the Kaan (*l. c.* vol. i, p. 360), he states that they "are most artfully covered with lion's skins, striped with black and white and red, ... a substance that lasts for ever. And inside they are all lined with *ermine* and *sable*, these two being the finest and most costly furs in existence." Odoric states (Yule's *Cathay*, vol. i, p. 130): "And all the walls [in the palace] are hung with skins of red leather, said to be the finest in the world." In the *Ku kuny i lu* (*Ji hia*, chap. xxxii, fol. 25) it is stated that in winter time the marquees (幕) of the principal hall were hung with *sleek leather* (油皮). Perhaps this is the fine leather Odoric means.

52. 紫檀 *Tze-t'an* is the name of a precious southern wood, very heavy and much prized even now in Peking. According to the *Yüan shi*, *Coubilaï khan* died in the *Tze-t'an tien* in February, 1294.

53. It seems that this surrounding gallery enclosed the principal hall and the three smaller halls above-mentioned. Compare map III.

"The gate 延春門 *Yen-ch'un men* is behind (*i. e.* to the north of) the *Pao-yün tien*. It is the principal gate leading to the hall *Yen-ch'un ko*; and has three gateways.

"The gate 懿範門 *I-fan men* is to the left (east) of the Yen-ch'un men; the gate 嘉則門 *Kia-tse men* to the right of it. (The *Kin pien* states, that these two gates were opposite the gates *Kia-k'ing men* and *King-fu men*). Both are of one gateway.

"The hall 延春閣 *Yen-ch'un ko* comprises nine *kien*. It measures 150 *ch'i* from east to west, is 90 *ch'i* in depth and 100 *ch'i* in height (thus higher than the Ta-ming tien. It was probably of two stories). The roof has threefold eaves. There is a pillared verandah (柱廊) 45 *ch'i* wide, 140 *ch'i* in depth, and 50 in height. To the hall belong, besides this, seven *kien* of dwelling-rooms, and four *kien* of other rooms, contiguous to the eastern and western ends of the building. Behind it is a 香閣 *Hiang-ko*.[54] I omit the detailed description of the Yen-ch'un ko. Imperial divans and thrones made of *tze t'an* (see note 52), 楠木 *nan-mu*,[55] and *camphor-wood* are mentioned there; also idols, etc.

"Two smaller halls are mentioned to the east and the west of the Yen-ch'un ko, viz. the 慈福殿 *Tze-fu tien*, called also 東煖殿 *Tung-nuan tien* (Eastern Winter hall), and the 明仁殿 *Ming-jen tien*, called also *Si-nuan tien* (Western Winter hall).

"The gate 景耀門 *King-yao men* is situated in the middle of the left (eastern) gallery; the 清灝門 *Ts'ing-hao men* in the middle of the right (western) gallery. A *bell-tower* stands south of King-yao men; a *drum-tower* south of Ts'ing-hao men. The gallery surrounding (the Yen-ch'un ko and the other halls) comprises a hundred and seventy-two *kien*. At each of the corners of this gallery is a tower (*lou*)."

It may be concluded from the above accounts of the *Ch'ue keng lu*, that the Mongol palace proper consisted of two divisions, both surrounded by a large gallery, and each containing one principal hall and several smaller ones. As in the corner of each of the galleried quadrangles was a tower, there were eight towers on the gallery. The Kung-ch'eng had also a tower in each corner; and, besides this, two towers are mentioned to the left and right of the Chang-t'ien men.

M. Polo states (*l. c.* vol. i, pp. 324, 325): "At each angle of the [outer palace] wall there is a very fine and rich palace, in which the war-harness of the Emperor is kept, such as bows and quivers, saddles

---

54. A similar building behind the Ta-ming tien was also mentioned. (See above.)

55. *Nan-mu* is the name of a precious Chinese wood, yielded by a tall tree belonging to a species of *Laurus*, and found in the Chinese provinces of *Sze-ch'uan*, *Hu-kuang*, etc. It is highly prized in China even at the present day.

and bridles, and bowstrings, and everything needful for an army. Also midway between every two of these Corner Palaces there is another of the like; so that taking the whole compass of the enclosure you find eight vast palaces stored with the Great Lord's harness of war ......[The second] enclosure also has eight palaces corresponding to those of the outer wall, and stored like them with the Lord's harness of war."

It seems to me that Polo took the towers mentioned by the Chinese author, in the angles of the galleries and of the Kung-ch'eng for palaces; for further on (p. 332) he states, that "over each gate [of Cambaluc] there is a great and handsome palace." I have little doubt that over the gates of Cambaluc, stood lofty buildings similar to those over the gates of modern Peking. These tower-like buildings are called *lou* by the Chinese, as I have stated above. It may be very likely, that at the time of M. Polo, the war-harness of the khan was stored in these towers of the palace wall. The author of the *Ch'ue keng lu*, who wrote more than 50 years later, assigns to it another place, as we shall see further on.

The same work describes, besides the above-mentioned, six other halls, all situated outside the *Ts'ing-hao men*. I omit the details, and as to their names, I beg the reader to refer to map III. All belonged to the *Ta-nei*, or the palace occupied by the khan, east of the lake. In the *Kin pien* (*Ji hia*, chap. xxx, fol. 1) this palace is called 慶福宮 *K'ing-fu kung*, and two other palaces are mentioned west of the lake, under the names of 興聖宮 *Hing-sheng kung* and 隆福宮 *Lung-fu kung*. Both are described also in the *Ch'ue keng lu*. I shall mention only such accounts of the Chinese authors as can be compared with Polo's statements.

Regarding the *Hing-sheng kung*, the *Ch'ue keng lu* states that it is situated to the north-west of the *Ta-nei*, west of the *Wan-sui shan* (see further on) and the lake; and that it is connected by a bridge with the eastern palace. At the time the author of the *Ch'ue keng lu* wrote, the Hing-sheng kung was occupied by empresses and concubines of the emperor. I omit the names of the halls, but shall notice the mentioning of a storehouse for *precious things* (藏珍庫), a storehouse for *saddles and bridles* (鞍轡庫), and a storehouse for the *war-harness* (軍器庫), in the Hing-sheng kung. M. Polo mentions the same storehouses, as situated in the khan's palace east of the lake. I may observe that at M. Polo's time the Hing-sheng palace did not yet exist. As is stated in the *Yüan shi* (annals), it was built in 1308.

As to the second palace, west of the lake, called *Lung-fu kung*, it is stated in the *Ch'ue kung lu*, that it lies west (opposite) of the Ta-nei and to the south of the Hing-sheng kung. This palace comprised seven halls, corresponding in their position, it seems, with the halls in the palace of the emperor; only they were smaller. At the time the *Ch'ue kung lu* was written, there were also empresses and concubines living in the Lung-fu kung.

In the *Yüan shi* (annals), chap. xviii, I find the following statement:—" In the 5th month of 1294 (i. e. four months after the death of Coubilaï), the palace where the empress lived, the same which in former times was the *residence* of the *heir-apparent*, received the name *Lung-fu kung* (改皇太后所居舊太子府爲隆福宮)."

M. Polo says (*l. c.* vol. i, p. 327): "You must know that beside the Palace (that we have been describing), *i. e.* the Great Palace, the Emperor has caused another to be built just like his own in every respect, and this he hath done for his son when he shall reign and be Emperor after him. . . . . . [It stands on the other side of the Lake from the Great Kaan's Palace, and there is a bridge crossing the water from one to the other.]"

Before quitting the description of the ancient palaces of Khanbaligh, let me mention a curious statement found in the *Ji hia*. In this work (chap. xxx, fol. 11), two authors of the Yüan dynasty are quoted, who report that Coubilaï khan, after having built the palaces in Peking, gave orders to bring from the 沙漠 *Sha-mo* (Mongolian desert), a kind of grass which the Chinese authors call 莎草 *so-ts'ao* or 青草 *ts'ing-ts'ao* (blue grass), and to cultivate it in the courts of the palace, that his sons and grandsons might not forget the steppes (草地), and that the emperor himself might always remember his modest origin. This grass was also called "the grass of the oath of moderation (誓 儉草)." The plant in question, according to the drawing in the Chinese botany *Chi wu ming shi t'u kao* chap. xxv, fol. 33 (a grass with bulbous roots is represented), seems to be a grass belonging to the Cyperaceous order.

M. Polo records (*l. c.* pp. 326,327): "From that corner of the enclosure [of the palace] which is towards the north-west there extends a fine Lake, containing foison of fish of different kinds. . . . . . A River enters this Lake and issues from it. . . . . . On the north side of the Palace, about a bowshot off, there is a hill which has been made by art [from the earth dug out of the Lake]; it is a good hundred paces in height and a mile in compass. This hill is entirely covered with trees that never lose their leaves, but remain ever green. And I assure you that wherever a beautiful tree may exist, and the Emperor gets news of it, he sends for it and has it transported bodily with all its roots and the earth attached to them, and planted on that hill of his . . . . . . And he has also caused the whole hill to be covered with the *ore of azure* (*roze de l'açur* in the Geog. Text), which is very green. And thus not only are the trees all green, but the hill itself is all green likewise ;. . . . hence it is called the *Green Mount*. . . . . . On the top of the hill again there is a fine big palace which is all green inside and out ; and thus the hill, and the trees, and the palace form together a charming spectacle. . . . . . .And the Great Kaan has caused this beautiful prospect to be formed for the comfort and solace and delectation of his heart."

Odoric; who visited Khanbaligh about thirty years after M. Polo left it, gives nearly the same description of the palace, the lake, the hill, etc.

Let me compare the Chinese statements about the same subject, recorded by authors of nearly M. Polo's and Odoric's time.

I may first observe that the lake which M. Polo saw, is the same as the 太液池 *T'ai-yi ch'i* of our days. It has, however, changed a little in its form. This lake and also its name *T'ai-yi ch'i* date from the 12th century, at which time an emperor of the Kin first gave orders to collect together the water of some springs in the hills, where now the summer palaces stand, and to conduct it to a place north of his capital, where pleasure gardens were laid out. The river, which enters the lake and issues from it exists still, under its ancient name 金水 *Kin-shui*. M. Polo's "Green Mount" is not as has been generally assumed by commentators, the present *King shan* north of the palace, but the above-mentioned *Pai-t'a shan* or *K'iung-hua tao*, north-west of the palace, as I shall show further on. It was an island in former times. The *Ch'uet keng lu*, chap. i, fol. 19, describes the lake, the hill, the palace on it etc, at the Mongol time, in the following terms :—[56]

"The 萬歲山 *Wan-sui shan* (Hill of Ten thousand years) lies to the north-west of the palace (*Ta-nei*), south of the *T'ai-yi ch'i* lake.[57] At the time of the Kin this hill was called the island of 瓊花 *K'iung-hua*.[58] In the year 1262 the (pleasure grounds on the) hill was repaired (by order of Coubilaï), and in 1271 it received the name *Wan-sui shan*. Elevations were made with 玲瓏石 *Ling-lung* stones,[59] piled up

---

56. Some particulars in my translation are taken from the description of the palaces in the *Ch'ue keng lu*, chap. xxi.
57. Further on the author states, that the lake extended also south of the hill as at present.
58. A name in use up to this time.
59. *Ling-lung*. These two characters, according to some of the Chinese dictionaries compiled by our sinologues, have only the meaning " sound of gems." This however is not the common meaning. Every Chinese knows, that *ling-lung* means " pierced or open work,"—what the French call "à jour." In the dictionary *Cheng tze t'ung*, *ling-lung* is explained by 彫鏤貌 "resembling cut work." *Ling-lung shi* is a general name for those large stones we see so often in Chinese gardens piled up with open interstices in artificial rocks and covered with moss and climbing plants. The stones are of very irregular shape, with sinuosities and hollows. It seems to me, that they belong to a kind of *tufaceous* limestone. The Chinese call them also 太湖石 *T'ai-hu shi* (stones from the lake *T'ai-hu*, near *Su-chou*, west of Shanghai). The Chinese say that this stone is found in that lake. Artificial rock-work of this kind can be seen in every Chinese garden, and of course also in the imperial gardens and on the *K'iung-hua tao*. Perhaps M. Polo, who states that the Green Mount was covered with " roze de l'açur " intended *roc* by " rze "

artificially into peaks. 松 *Sung* and 檜 *kui* trees[60] were planted, and thus the whole hill is covered with a splendid vegetation, and all has the appearance of a natural hill. To the east of the hill, there is a stone bridge 76 *ch'i* long and 41 broad. In the middle of the bridge is an aqueduct, which leads the water of the 金水 *Kin-shui* to the top of the hill. For the water from the *Kin-shui* has been conducted behind the hill, and it is pumped by means of machines to the top of it,[61] where it pours forth from the mouth of a stone dragon, into a square basin. Thence it runs concealed to the northern side of the hall *Jen-chi tien* (see further on). There is a twining dragon with his head aloft, which vomits water. Then the water runs from east to west and is discharged into the lake *T'ai-yi ch'i*.

"On the top of the *Wan-sui shan*, there is the hall 廣寒殿 *Kuang-han tien*, comprising seven *kien*. It measures 120 *ch'i* from east to west, 62 in depth, and 50 in height.[62] There is a jar of black jade for wine (黑玉酒甕一). This jade has white veins, and in accordance with these veins, fish and animals have been carved on the jar. The jar is big enough to hold more than 30 piculs of wine.[63] There is also an artificial hill made of jade, and many other curiosities mentioned in or about the *Kuang-han tien*.

"The hall 仁智殿 *Jen-chi tien* is situated between the top and the foot of the hill and comprises three *kien*.

"The lake *T'ai-yi ch'i*, which is west of the *Ta-nei* (Palace of the emperor), is several *li* in circuit. (The *Ku kung i lu*, quoted in the *Ji hia*, chap. xxxii, fol. 26, states that the lake 海子 *Hai-tze* west of the *Ta-nei* has an extent of 5 or 6 *li*.)

"The hall 儀天殿 *I-t'ien tien* is situated on a round islet in the lake, directly opposite the *Wan-sui shan*. It has eleven pillars, is 35 feet high and 70 *ch'i* in circuit. There is a compartment for the life-guards.

---

and *à jour* by "*neur.*" This is however an hypothesis I venture without laying any stress upon it. An author of the beginning of the 15th century, quoted in the *Ji hia*, chap. xxxvi. fol. 12, states that the earth for piling up the K'iung-hua tao was brought from outside the northern frontier (see further on, the report of the *Ch'ue keng lu* regarding this tradition), but that the stones with which it is covered were brought from 艮嶽 *Ken-yo*. Ken-yo was the name of a hill in the north-eastern corner of the city of 汴梁 *Pien-liang*, the present K'ai-feng fu (see Yi *t'ung chi*).

60. *Sung* is the Chinese name for "pine;" *kui* is "Juniperus Chinensis (see my *Notes on Chinese Mediæval travellers*, p. 123). Even now the K'iung-hua tao is covered with beautiful groves of evergreen trees, namely *Pinus Massoniana*, the white-barked *Pinus Bungeana* and *Juniperus Chinensis*, which is also a tall tree.
61. There is still a canal with a bridge over it, east of the K'iung-hua tao, according to the Chinese maps. This canal separates it from the shore. As the K'iung-hua tao belongs to the prohibited grounds, I cannot speak from my own observation.
62. I have no doubt that M. Polo's handsome palace on the top of the Green Mount is the same as the *Kuang-han tien* of the Chinese author.
63. There is still a large jar of jade 4 *ch'i* 5 *ts'un* in diameter, 2 *ch'i* in height, and 15 *ch'i* in circuit, kept in a pavilion near the *Ch'eng-kuang tien* (south of the K'iung-hua tao), according to Chinese works. The *Ji hia* (chap. xxv, fol. 23, 25) states that it has been preserved from the time of the Kin and the Yüan.

A marble bridge, 200 *ch'i* long, connects this island with the *Wan-sui shan*. Another bridge, made of wood, 120 *ch'i* long and 22 broad, leads eastward to the wall of the imperial palace. A third bridge, a wooden drawbridge (木吊橋) 470 *ch'i* long, stretches to the west over the lake to its western border, where the palace 興聖宮 *Hing-sheng kung* (see above) stands. When the emperor goes to 上都 *Shang-tu* (his summer residence), the two boats in the middle of this bridge are taken out, and the thoroughfare is interrupted.⁶⁴

"To the east of the *Wan-sui shan* lies the 靈囿 *Ling yu* or "Divine park," in which rare birds and beasts are kept.⁶⁵ Before the emperor goes to *Shang-tu*, the officers are accustomed to be entertained at this place.

"The governor of the Chekiang province, by name *Ch'i-te-rh* (evidently a Mongol name) told me (i. e. the author of the *Ch'ue keng lu*) that at the time he was *Liu-shou-sze* (governor) of *Ta-tu* (Khanbaligh) he heard from old men the following tradition about the *Wan-sui shan*: —"People say, that at about the rise of the Mongol dynasty in the 朔漠 *So-mo* (Northern desert), there was at the northern frontier, a

---

64. The *Ku kung i lu* (*Ji lia*, chap. xxxii, fol. 26) calls the island where the three bridges meet, 瀛洲 *Ying-chou* "Fairy island," and states that on it was a round hall (圓殿), surrounded by a stone wall. This wall of the Yüan time still exists. It is known under the name of 圓城 *Yüan-ch'eng* (round wall), and surrounds the hall 承光殿 *Ch'eng-kuang tien*, situated at the eastern end of the large marble bridge crossing the lake. This hall is the same as the *I-t'ien tien* of the Yüan. The name was changed during the Ming, as the *Ch'un ming meng yü lu* reports (chap. vi, fol. 16). Thus this identification leaves no doubt. Now however this round wall and the hall inside stand, not on an island as in the Mongol time, but on a projection of the eastern shore. This projection is connected by a beautiful marble bridge with the *K'iung-hua tao*. I am not aware whether it is the same marble bridge as mentioned in the *Ch'ue keng lu* at the same place. M. Polo's bridge, crossing the lake from one side to the other, must be identified with the wooden bridge mentioned in the *Ch'ue keng lu*. The present marble bridge spanning the lake was only built in 1392 (*Ch'un ming meng yü lu*, chap. vi, fol. 9). It seems that the lake, in the time of the Mongols extended more to the east than now, and that in the beginning of the 13th century, the K'iung-hua tao was in the middle of the lake. Let me quote what the *Si yu ki* (see my notes on *Chinese Medieval Travellers*) says regarding the lake and the K'iung-hua tao. After *Ch'ang-ch'un* had returned from western Asia (1224) he lived some years in Peking; and, as the narrative states, the ground of the gardens of the northern palace (of the Kin) was given to him (by order of Tchingiz khan) for the purpose of establishing there a Taouist monastery. Further on it is said, that this monastery was on the *K'iung-hua* island, and that it was forbidden to the people to gather fuel in the park of the island, and to fish in the lake. (I may observe, that at that time this ground was not inside the capital but north of it.) *Ch'ang-ch'un* sometimes took a walk to the top of the hill 壽樂山 *Show-le shan* (it seems the top of the K'iung-hua tao is meant), and enjoyed the magnificent view he had of the surrounding gardens. Further on we read :—"On the 23rd of the 6th month (June) 1227 it was reported to the master, that owing to the heavy rains, the southern embankment of the lake *T'ai-yi ch'i* had fallen down ; and that the water had gushed into the *eastern lake*, so that it was heard at a distance of several *li*. After this all fish and tortoises disappeared, and the lake became dry". *Ch'ang ch'un* took this for an omen of his death, and indeed he died some months after.

65. This park is mentioned by M. Polo as well as by Odoric as a park with "beasts also of sundry kinds, such as white stags and fallow deer, gazelles and roebucks, and fine squirrels of various sorts, with numbers also of the animal that gives the musk, and all manner of other beautiful creatures." *M. Polo l. c.* vol. i, p. 326. Yule's *Cathay*, vol. i, p. 129.)

certain hill with very powerful properties. A fortune-teller of the *Kin* reported, that the supremacy depended upon the possession of this hill, and that it was not advantageous for the *Kin* that the hill should be in the power of the Mongols. Thereupon the *Kin* made an agreement with the Mongols, engaging themselves to pay tribute, making only the condition to have the hill, in order to strengthen their power in their own country. The Mongols laughed and did not make any objection to this condition. Then the *Kin* arrived with their soldiers, dug down the hill, laded the earth on carts and carried it to the city of 幽州 *Yu chou*.[66] North of the city they piled up the earth. Thus a hill was formed, around which a lake was dug, gardens were laid out there, palaces were built, and it became a pleasure ground. After *Shi-tsu* (Coubilaï khan) had destroyed the *Kin* dynasty, he built his palace here in 1267, and the (K'iung-hua tao) hill was then enclosed in the palace grounds. In 1271 the ancient name of K'iung-hua ao was changed into *Wan-sui shan*.[67]

I have no doubt, that the " Green Mount " of M. Polo and Odoric is the same as the *K'iung-hua tao*. Their descriptions agree well with the statements regarding this hill of the contemporary Chinese authors; and in the *Kin pien* (*Ji hia*, chap. xxx, fol. 2) a "green rock" (翠 巖) is mentioned in connection with the *Wan-sui shan* or *K'iung-hua tao*. The *Ku kung i lu* (*Ji hia*, chap. xxxii, fol. 26) in describing the *Wan-sui shan*, praises the beautiful shady green of the vegetation there (幽 芳翠草).

---

66. This was the name of Peking in the time of the T'ang dynasty.
67. This tradition regarding the origin of the K'iung-hua tao is perhaps older than the *Ch'ue keng lu* alleges ; for some ancient authors state (*Ji hia*, chap. xxix, fol. 20) that already in the time of the *Liao* this island existed, and that the famed empress *Siao* (see note 23), had a palace there (梳粧樓 or " Toilet tower " in the literal translation). In the Biography of *Bardja Arte Tegin*, king of the *Ouigours* (Bardjoui of Rashid-eddin) in the *Yüen shi*, chap. cxxii, a similar legend is circumstantially related regarding a hill of Mongolia, carried away by the Chinese. As the translation of that biography, by Visdelou, is found in the *Suppl. à la Bibl. Orient.* p. 138, and also in Klaproth's *Mém. rel. à l'Asie*, tom. ii, pp. 332-336 (see also *D'Ohsson, l. c.* tom. i, p. 438), I will only say a few words regarding it. According to this tradition, which seems to originate with the Ouigours, at the time of the *T'ang* dynasty, in the 8th century, the Chinese were desirous of being on good terms with the Ouigours, who were then a powerful nation in Mongolia, and had their capital near the place where afterwards Caracorum was built. A Chinese princess was given in marriage to a Ouigour prince, and afterwards a Chinese envoy was sent to the Ouigour capital. When he arrived at the frontier he was told, that near 和林 *Ho-lin* (afterwards Caracorum) there was a hill, called the "Hill of happiness," and that the supremacy depended on the possession of this hill. If the T'ang could destroy it, the power of the Ouigours would be broken. The Chinese envoy therefore asked from the Ouigour khan, as price for the Chinese princess given in marriage, only this " Hill of happiness." The khan agreed. But as the hill was big, the Chinese made a great fire around, and then poured vinegar on it. After it had been broken into pieces, it was placed on carts and carried away to China. I am not disinclined to melt together this Ouigour tradition with the Chinese one regarding the K'iung-hua tao, but as to their authenticity I confess some scepticism. Some cart-loads of earth from a hill in Mongolia may have been brought to Peking; but it seems to me more rational to assume, that the greater part of the earth forming the K'iung-hua tao, was obtained by digging the lake.

The commentators of M. Polo generally identify the Green Mount of the traveller with the *King shan*, which stands opposite the palace, north of it, and about ¾ *li* distant to the east from the *K'iung-hua tao*. Indeed M. Polo says that the Green Mount was north of the palace about a bowshot off. But as the Wan-sui shan is the only hill mentioned by the Chinese authors of the Mongol time on the palace grounds, we can only identify this hill with the Green Mount.

I am inclined to suppose, that the *King shan* did not exist at the time of the Mongols. It seems that in Chinese books mention is first made of this hill at the end of the 16th century. Nothing is said in the *Ji hia* of its earlier history or its origin. I read in Col. Yule's *M. Polo*, vol. i, p. 330, that according to Dr. Lockhart the King shan was formed by the Ming emperors from the excavation of the existing lake. I am not aware where Dr. Lockhart found this statement. Perhaps he may be right. The drawing Yule gives of the King shan resembles as much this hill as it does the Calton hill at Edinburgh. Evidently he has copied a drawing invented somewhere in Europe.

The King shan is not a cone as represented in that drawing, but it has an oblong form, stretching from east to west. The hill has five peaks crowned with pavilions and is visible from all sides.

The present name of the hill 景山 *King shan* (Prospect hill) dates only from the present dynasty. The authors of the Ming mention it under the name of *Wan-sui shan*; the same name as the *K'iung-hua tao* had in the time of the Mongols. Its popular name was formerly as it is now 煤山 *Mei shan*. The *Ji hia* states (chap. xxxv, fol. 16,17), that at first, during the Yüan, by the name of *Wan-sui shan*, the *K'iung-hua tao* was always understood. But since the time of 馬仲房 (evidently an author of the Ming), the name Wan-sui shan was also applied to the *Mei shan*, and that thereupon a great confusion resulted. Indeed many authors of the Ming confound the two hills. The *Ji hia*, which distinguishes them clearly, says[68] that the name of *Mei shan* (Coal hill) was given to it from the stock of coal buried at its foot, as a provision in case of siege. Nothing is said there about the hill being composed of coal as Col. Yule states, I do not know on what authority. The *Ji hia* says further, that this hill was the protecting hill of the imperial palace (大內之鎮山) in the time of the Ming.[69] It was measured by imperial order in 1634, and found to be 147 *ch'i* high.[70] The Mei shan has a sad historical celebrity. The last

---

68. On the authority of the 野獲編 *Ye hu pien*, a work published under the Ming.
69. The hill is situated just in the middle of the Tartar city according to the survey of the French astronomers.
70. I estimate the Mei shan at about 200 feet. The K'iung-hua tao may be 100 feet in height. The modern Chinese authors give to the K'iung-hua tao 1½ *li* in circuit. M. Polo's Green Mount was "a good hundred paces in height and a mile in compass."

emperor of the *Ming* hanged himself on a 海棠 *hai-t'ang* (crab-apple) tree, in the park of the hill, in 1644, when the Manchoos had taken the capital.[71]

ON THE WATER CONVEYANCES CONNECTING PEKING IN ANCIENT TIMES WITH THE GREAT RIVER SYSTEM OF CHINA.

Everybody has heard of the *Grand Canal* of China, connecting the capital with the large rivers of the empire. The Grand Canal, —in Chinese 御河 *Yü ho* (Imperial river), also 運河 *Yün ho*, or 運糧河 *Yün-liang ho* (river for the transport of corn), has its extremities at *Peking* and at *Hang-chou fu* in Chekiang. This canal, as may be seen on the maps, has a general direction from north to south, or to the south-east; and the waters of all the rivers it meets in its course, have been made to flow in the same channel. In parts it follows for some extent the course of natural rivers; f. i. the 白河 *Pai ho* (Pei ho) and the 衛河 *Wei ho* in the north, which for a long distance form the Grand Canal. It crosses the largest rivers of China, the 黃河 *Huang ho* and the 大江 *Ta kiang* (more generally known to Europeans under the name of *Yang-tze kiang*[72]), and also the 淮水 *Huai shui*. In ancient times the Grand Canal was of the greatest importance to trade, and for supplying the capital with rice. But now this great watercourse has only an importance for the capital as regards its northern part, between *T'ientsin* and *Peking;* and I have been told, that owing to the carelessness of the government in keeping it in repair, it is only partly navigable south of T'ientsin. This would explain the extraordinary fact, that the conservative Chinese,—who do not generally adopt the great inventions of the west, —some years ago established a Chinese steam-ship company, for carrying the rice indispensable to the capital, from the southern provinces to T'ientsin.

According to Father Hyacinth *(Statist. Description of China*, in Russian, vol. ii, p. 188), the part of the Grand Canal between the Yellow river and the Yang-tze kiang was constructed more than five hundred years before our era. Klaproth states *(Mémoires relatifs à l'Asie*, tom. iii, p. 318), that the construction of the southern part of the canal, between Chin-kiang fu and Hang-chou fu, dates from the

---

71. Interesting details regarding this event are found in the 3rd volume of the *Records of the Russian Ecclesiastical Mission in Peking*, p. 56, in Khropowitzky's article, "The fall of the Ming dynasty."

72. The latter name 揚子江 *Yang-tze kiang* is not frequently seen in Chinese books, and on Chinese maps we generally find the river termed *Ta kiang*, meaning the "Great river." I fancy Yang-tze kiang is only a popular name of the river near its mouth; for the first character *yang* is the ancient name of a Chinese province comprising the present Kiangsu, Chekiang and Anhui. The ancient Jesuit missionaries, who probably had not seen the name written, translated it erroneously by "Son of the Ocean" (comp. Du Halde). Marco Polo calls the Yang-tze the "Great River *Kian*" (l. c. vol. ii, p. 132).

beginning of the 7th century of our era. It is generally believed that Coubilaï khan first constructed the northern part of the Grand Canal, connecting Peking with the Yellow river (Klaproth, l. c.). But, as can be proved from ancient Chinese works, water conveyance between Peking and the provinces south of the capital existed much earlier; and it seems, since Peking had become an imperial residence, the emperors had taken care to connect the capital by water with the provinces rich in corn. As to the *Liao*, who first made Peking a capital, the dominions of that dynasty spread to the south only as far as 200 *li* beyond Peking. But according to the *Ti king king wu lio (Ji hia*, chap. xciv, fol. 1), in the time of the empress *Siao* (see above, note 23), there was a *Yün-liang ho*, or river for the transport of corn, leading to the capital. I observe that the *Hun ho* river as well as the *Pai ho*, from their sources to their mouths belonged to the Liao empire. The *Kin*, who superseded the Liao, A. D. 1115, succeeded in enlarging their dominions to the south as far as the *Huai* river. In the *Kin shi*, or "History of the Kin," we find a detailed description of a canal connecting the capital with the provinces of *Ho-pei* and *Shan-tung* (see note 78).

Before entering into particulars regarding the ancient canal system of northern China, I may be allowed to say a few words about the present water system of the Peking plain; for the watercourses there have much changed since those ancient times; or I should rather say, the rivers have reverted to their original channels, after having been forced for a long time to send their waters to the capital.

The plain is irrigated by two rivers and their affluents. The 渾河 *Hun ho* (muddy river), after emerging from the western mountains, passes about seven English miles west of Peking. The 白河 *Pai ho* ("White river:"—on our maps the name is generally written *Pe ho*), which comes from the north, is at the nearest point *(T'ung chou)* thirteen English miles distant from the capital. The Hun ho discharges itself into the Pai ho near T'ientsin, where also the *Wei* river from the south, or the Grand Canal, unites its waters with those of the Pai ho.

One of the principal tributaries of the Pai ho from the west is the 沙河 *Sha ho* (Sand river). This river is composed of a number of smaller streams, the sources of which lie in the northern and western mountains. These confluents are often exhausted during the dry season. The most important of them are known under the names of 南沙河 *Nan sha ho*, and 北沙河 *Pei sha ho* (Southern and Northern Sha ho), the latter is termed also 溪河 *K'i ho* on Chinese maps. The large village of *Sha-ho*, and the ruins of an ancient city of the same name are situated in the angle, where the Pei sha ho and Nan sha ho unite. A third confluent coming from the north, from a hill north of the village of 白浮 *Po-fou*, discharges itself into the Pei sha ho near the same place. Three ancient stone bridges span the three rivers.[73] The great highway from Peking to Kalgan passes through the village of Sha-ho. Compare map IV.

Further on in its course, the Sha ho receives the river 清河 Ts'ing ho, which issues from the lake 昆明湖 K'un-ming hu, near the summer palaces. The Sha ho finally empties itself into the Pai ho, a little east of T'ung chou; but before entering the Pai-ho, it receives from the west the waters coming from the capital.

The irrigation of Peking is effected now in the following manner. Five or six miles to the north-west of the capital is the above-mentioned lake K'un-ming hu, around which the summer palaces are situated. It may be four miles or more in circuit, and is filled by some copious springs on the adjacent hill 玉泉山 Yü-ts'üan shan. A canal has been conducted from this lake to Peking. The water arrives at the north-western corner of the capital, and expands near the bridge 高梁橋 Kao-liang k'iao (see map 1) into a little reservoir, from which one part issues to supply the moat of Peking, while another part enters the Tartar city and forms a large reservoir, extending from the northern wall of Peking to the northern wall of the Imperial city. These reservoirs are called 積水潭 Tsi-shui t'an[74] (meaning reservoir). Further on the water has been introduced by a canal into the Imperial city, where it expands again and forms the lake T'ai-yi chi already mentioned. After flowing through the prohibited city, the water issues from it in the south-eastern corner. The canal passes before the British legation, and running southward, passes through the southern city wall, where it discharges its water into the southern moat of the Tartar city. At the south-eastern corner of that city, near the bridge 大通橋 Ta-t'ung k'iao (see map 1), all the water passing through and around Peking unites and forms the beginning of the Grand Canal. This part of the canal, running straight to T'ung chou (40 li east of Peking), is known to Europeans under the name of T'ung-chou canal, but it is called 大通河 Ta-t'ung ho, or 通惠河 T'ung-hui ho by the Chinese, and was known by the latter name as early as the 13th century.

Besides the lake K'un-ming hu, the T'ung-chou canal receives water from two other sources.

At the south-western corner of the Tartar city, the small river 三里河 San-li ho, discharges itself into the moat. It commences at the present day 1½ English mile north-west of that place, at a little lake named from the 望海樓 Wang-hai lou. On the bord-

---

73. One of these stone bridges is stated in the *Chang an k'o hua*, chap. IV, fol. 30, to have been constructed between A. D. 1436 and 1450.
74. They are mentioned under the same name in the history of the Mongol dynasty.

er of the lake there is an imperial palace, and a pleasure ground called 釣魚臺 *Tiao-yü t'ai* (Terrace for angling). There was an imperial pleasure ground there as early as the 12th century (*Ji hia*, chap. xcv, fol. 7). I remember the time, when the Peking races took place in the dry bed of this lake. But during the last four or five years it has been filled with water again. We shall see further on, that the *San-li ho* was an important river in ancient times, and passed between the Mongol capital and the ancient capital of the Kin.

Proceeding on the stone road from the gate *Chang-yi men* (of the Chinese city), about 4½ *li* to the south-west, we see to the right a square rampart, about 4 *li* in circuit. It encloses a pond called 蓮花池 *Lien-hua ch'i* (Lotus pond) by the Chinese. The water issuing from it runs to the south-east, discharges into the moat of the Chinese city, and thus also reaches the T'ung-chou canal near the bridge Ta-t'ung k'iao. It seems that in ancient times, the water from the Lotus pond flowed through the capital of the Kin.

Below T'ung-chou the Pai ho receives from the west the water of the river 涼水 *Liang shui*. This river is formed by two confluents, which take rise in the marshes south-west of the Chinese city. The northern one, as we have seen, formed in ancient time, the southern moat of the Kin capital. The two rivers unite south of the Chinese city; the water then enters the park *Nan-hai-tzi*, issues from it through its eastern wall, and reaches the Pai ho near the village of 張家灣 *Chang-kia wan*.

After this short sketch of the watercourses in the Peking plain, let me show what the ancient Chinese books record regarding the water conveyances leading to Peking.

In the history of the Kin dynasty, a whole chapter is devoted to the description of the rivers and canals of the empire (*Kin shi*, chap. xxvii, 河渠). Under the heads of 漕渠 (Canal for the transport of corn) and 盧蒲河 (the same as the *Hun ho*, as we shall see further on), I find the following statements:—

"*Yen* (the capital of the Kin:—see above), is distant from the 潞水 *Lu shui*[75] 50 *li*. The 高梁河 *Kao-liang ho*,[76] and the water of the 白蓮潭 *Po-lien t'an* (Pool of the White Lotus[77]), have been employed for the canal (leading to the Lu shui). Sluices have been established; by means of which it is possible to reach by water the provinces

---

75. *Lu shui* is the ancient name of the *Pai ho*. In the *Yüan shi*, chap. lxiv, art. Pai ho, it is stated:—"There are three rivers important for the Transport canal, the 白河 *Pai ho*, the 榆河 *Yü ho* and the 渾河 *Hun ho*. These rivers unite and then take the name of 潞水 *Lu shui*." In works anterior to the *Yüan shi* however, the Pai ho, is always termed *Lu shui*.
76. *Kao-liang ho*, an ancient river somewhere near the present *Si-chi men*; at least the bridge near this gate is still called *Kao-liang k'iao*.
77. Perhaps the same as the above-mentioned *Lotus pond*, west of the Chinese city.

of Shantung and 河北 *Ho-pei*.⁷⁸ At the cities situated on this waterway granaries have been established; so that the corn can arrive at the capital by water." I omit the detailed description of the water communications of the capital with the provinces south of it; and will only say, that from the rivers and cities named, it may be concluded, that the principal watercourse at the time of the Kin was by the *Pai ho*, and the 衞河 *Wei ho* which discharges itself into the Pai ho near T'ientsin. Thus the Grand Canal,—said to have been first constructed by the Mongols,—existed for the greater part before the Mongols arrived; at least it is certain, that the principal Transport canal of the Kin between the capital and *Lin-ts'ing chou* (on the Wei river), followed the same course as that of the Grand Canal at the present day.

The *Kin shi* states further, that between *T'ung chou* and the capital there were some difficulties in the navigation; T'ung chou being too elevated with respect to the capital. The water therefore flowed down very slowly, and the canal was often obstructed by mud. In the year A. D. 1170, a proposition was made to the emperor to introduce water from the *Lu-kou* river (the *Hun ho*,—see above), into the Transport canal. It had been ascertained, that the 金口 *Kin k'ou*,⁷⁹ was 140 feet higher than the capital; and by this means a more rapid current might be expected for the Transport canal. The emperor was much delighted by this project, and orders were given for its execution. A canal was dug from the *Kin k'ou* to the northern moat of the capital, whence it was conducted to the *Lu* river. It reached the river north (probably a misprint for south) of T'ung chou. The whole work was finished in fifty days. But the result did not answer the expectation. Sometimes the water ran too rapidly and the embankments fell down; at other times the water deposited much mud and formed sands. In A. D. 1175, the Lu kou river broke through the embankments near the village of 上陽村 *Shang-yang ts'un* (Upper village of *Yang*).

In the annals of the *Kin shi*, under the year 1186 it is stated, that one of the ministers drew the attention of the emperor to the fact, that the *Kin k'ou* being 140 feet higher than the capital, there would be great danger if an inundation should happen. He proposed to shut up the canal (connecting with the Lu kou river); to which the emperor agreed.

In the *Yüan shi*, chap. clxiv, Biography of *Kuo Shou-king*,⁸⁰ it is

---

78. The province of *Ho-pei* at the time of the Kin, comprised the southern part of the present Chili, a part of *Shantung*, and the portion of the present *Honan* situated north of the Yellow river.

79. *Kin k'ou* is still the name for the passage north of the 石景山 *Shi-king shan*, an isolated hill near the place where the Hun ho emerges into the plain.

80. 郭守敬 *Kuo Shou-king*, the celebrated engineer of Coubilai khan, especially famed for the gigantic water-works he executed. He constructed also the Grand Canal.

recorded that in the year A. D. 1265, this high officer made the following report to the emperor:—"At the time of the Kin there was a canal led off from the *Hun ho* eastward. It began at the village of 麻峪 *Ma-yü*,[81] and passed through the *Kin k'ou*. Its water irrigated the fields north of *Yen king* (the capital of the Kin) to an extent of nearly 1000 *k'ing*.[82] But owing to a war which had broken out, the canal was shut up at Kin k'ou with big stones. Kuo Shou-king now proposed to open this canal again, in order that the environs of the capital should enjoy the benefit of the water. But to prevent the danger which might arise from sudden freshets, he formed a project to dig another canal to the south-west, which should turn around the Hun ho." According to the *Yüan shi*, Annals, this project was executed in 1266, and the opened canal (to the capital) was afterwards used for carrying stones and wood (from the western hills). But as we shall see further on, this canal was shut up again, owing to heavy inundations threatening the capital, at the end of the 13th century.

Let me show what the *Yüan shi* reports concerning the *T'ung-hui ho*, or as we call it, the *T'ung-chou* canal, connecting Peking with T'ung chou (see *Yüan shi*, chap. lxiv, on the water systems,—and clxiv, Biography of Kuo Shou-king):—

"The 通惠河 *T'ung-hui ho* takes its rise from the 白浮 *Po-fou* springs and those of the 甕山 *Weng shan*. In the year 1291, the inspector general of the water conveyances, Kuo Shou-king, received orders to unite the rivers (in the neighborhood of Peking), and utilize their water for navigation. Kuo Shou-king made a proposal to dig a canal from T'ung chou to the capital (it is not clearly stated whether a new canal), and to use the water of the Hun ho only for irrigating the fields (he speaks evidently of the Hun ho canal, opened in 1266). He proposed to lead fresh water into the ancient bed of the 㶟河 *Ch'a ho*.[83] The fresh water was led off from the springs on the hill 神山 *Shen shan* near the village 白浮 *Po-fou*, belonging to 昌平縣 *Ch'ang-p'ing hien* (now *Ch'ang-p'ing chou*).[84] The canal went at first westward and then turned to the south, crossed the rivers 雙塔河 *Shuang-t'a ho* and 榆河 *Yü ho*,[85] and passing the springs 一畝泉 *Yi-mu ts'üan*

---

81. *Ma-yü* is still the name of a village situated on the left bank of the Hun ho, north of the Shi-king shan and near the Kin k'ou.
82. A 頃 *k'ing* is = 100 畝 *mou*. 6.6 *mou* = 1 English acre.
83. Literally the "River provided with sluices." He means probably the river, or canal, carrying the water from the *K'un-ming* lake to the capital.
84. The village *Po-fou* still exists south-east of Ch'ang-p'ing chou. My friend Dr. von Möllendorff, of the German Legation, has visited the place, and I am indebted to him for some information regarding it. North of the village is an isolated hill (probably the *Shen shan* of the *Yüan shi*) from which a river comes down and runs to the south, discharging itself into the *Pei sha ho*, near the village of *Sha-ho* (see map IV).
85. Further on the *Yüan shi* states, that the *Shuang-t'a ho* is an affluent of the *Yü ho*. The *Ji hia*, chap. cxxxiv, fol. 18, identifies the *Yü ho* with the *Pei sha ho* (see above).

and 玉泉 *Yü ts'üan*[86] (carrying their waters along), ran through the 甕山泊 *Weng-shan* lake,[87] and reached the capital near the western gate. The canal entered the city, formed a reservoir to the south called 積水潭 *Tsi-shui t'an*,[88] ran to the south-east (through the capital), and issued east of the gate 文明門 *Wen-ming men*.[89] Further on it entered the ancient Transport canal,[90] reached the village of 高麗莊 *Kao-li chuang* belonging to T'ung chou,[91] and finally discharged itself into the 白河 *Pai ho*. The length of the whole canal from the Shen shan to T'ung chou was 164 *li* and 104 *pu*. The work was begun in spring 1292 and finished next year in autumn, nineteen thousand soldiers having been employed on it. The canal was named T'ung-hui, being very useful for the transport of corn." The *Yüan shi* then enumerates all the sluices of the canal. One was outside the 和義門 *Ho-yi men* (answering to the present *Si-chi men* gate:—see map I), at the distance of one *li* to the north-west; the next was at the *Ho-yi men* itself. One sluice was inside the city, at the 海子 *Hai-tze* (the lake near the palace); one was outside of 麗正門 *Li-cheng men*, to the south-east of the water-gate (through the wall) of the canal; the next, one *li* to the south-west of *Wen-ming men*; the next, one *li* to the south-east of it; the next, one *li* further to the east. Four sluices are enumerated on the canal leading from the capital to T'ung chou. It is stated that the canal passed through T'ung chou (as at present), —that it entered near the western gate, and issued near the southern. As I have shown, the T'ung-chou canal does not now flow directly into the *Pai ho*, but discharges itself into the *Sha ho*, which at a short distance more to the east enters the Pai ho.

The reader will observe in comparing my maps representing modern Peking, its environs, and the present canal and river system, that the course of the water running from the lake *K'un-ming hu* through Peking to T'ung chou, has not changed since the time of the Mongols. But the canal from the *Po-fou* sources to the K'un-ming hu does not exist at the present time, and the rivers, the water of

---

86. The *Yü ts'üan* is the water coming out from the hill 玉泉山 *Yü-ts'üan shan* (see map IV).
87. *Weng-shan* is the original name of the hill situated north of the lake *K'un-ming hu*, better known now under the name of 萬壽山 *Wan-shou shan*. The *Weng-shan* lake, the same as the K'un-ming hu of our days, is called 七里灣 *Ts'i-li wan* (the beach of seven *li*) in the *Ch'un ving meng yü lu* (*Ji hia*, chap. lxxxix, fol. 9).
88. The reservoir has the same name at the present time.
89. The *Wen-ming* gate answers to the *Ha-ta men* of modern Peking. "East of the gate" is a misprint for "west;" for it results from the enumeration of the sluices the *Yüan shi* gives further on, that the canal issued west of the Wen-ming gate, as it does now.
90. 入舊運糧河. It seems that the Transport canal of the Kin from the capital to T'ung chou, was the same as the *T'ung-hui ho* of the Yüan, and that the Mongols only repaired the canal of the Kin.
91. I inquired in T'ung chou about *Kao-li chuang*. It seems that no village of this name exists at the present time.

which had been introduced into it, have taken their original direct course to the *Pai ho*. The *Ji hia*, chap. lxxxix, fol. 7, quotes an author of the Ming, who states, that since the Mongol period the course of the rivers has changed, and that the canal leading water from the north to the lake (K'un-ming hu), has been obstructed north of the *Weng-shan* (Wan-shou shan:—see above).

It is not without interest to compare these ancient Chinese statements as above related, with what Rashid-eddin reports regarding the Transport canal connecting Khanbaligh with the principal cities of China (Yule's *Cathay*, vol. ii, pp. 258,259):—

"Two important rivers pass by *Khanbaligh* and *Daïdu*. After coming from the direction of the Kaan's summer residence in the north, and flowing near *Jamjál*, they unite to form another river.[92] A very large basin, like a lake in fact, has been dug near the city and furnished with a slip for launching pleasure boats. The river had formerly another channel, and discharged itself into the gulf of the ocean, which penetrated within a short distance of Khanbaligh. But in the course of time this channel had become so shallow as not to admit the entrance of shipping, so that they had to discharge their cargoes and send them up to Khanbaligh on pack-cattle. And the Chinese engineers and men of science having reported that the vessels from the provinces of Cathay, from the capital of MACHIN (Canton, according to Yule), and from cities of KHINGSAÏ (Hang-chou fu) and ZAITON (without doubt Ts'üan-chou fu) no longer could reach the metropolis, the Khan gave them orders to dig a great canal, into which the waters of the said river and of several others should be introduced. This canal extends for a distance of forty days' navigation from Khanbaligh to Khingsai and Zaitun......The canal is provided with many sluices intended to distribute the water over the country......"

We have seen, that a part of the water of the *Hun ho* had been conducted in the time of the Kin, to the capital and into the Transport canal, and that the Hun-ho canal had afterwards been shut up, but had been opened again during the reign of Coubilaï, who in 1298 gave orders to shut it again, owing to inundations threatening the capital. In the middle of the 14th century the Hun ho question was brought upon

---

92. Rashid-eddin's accounts regarding the rivers is a little confused, and it is difficult to say which of the rivers of the Peking plain he means. The 北沙河 *Pei sha ho* or 溪河 *K'i ho* comes down from the defile of 居庸 *Kü-yung*, where the direct way to Shang-tu, the summer residence of the Mongol khans, passed through. *Jamjál* therefore may be identified with the defile of *Kü-yung*. In the Mongol text of the *Yüan ch'ao pi shi*, written in 1240 (see my *Notes on Chinese Mediæval Travellers*, p. 110), this defile is repeatedly mentioned and always termed *Jahjal*. I may observe, that Rashid in rendering the Chinese name for the summer residence *K'ai-p'ing fu* spells the name *K'ai-min fu*, thus substituting there also an *m* for a *p*.

the *tapis* once more. The *Ji hia* (chap. civ, fol. 17), quotes the following statements from the *Yüan shi* regarding this subject:—

"In the year A. D. 1342, one of the ministers proposed to the emperor to dig a new canal, 50 feet deep and 20 feet broad, from the village of *Kao-li chuang*, south of T'ung chou (see note 91), to the *Kin k'ou* (see note 79) in the Western mountains, and to remove the iron lock by which the ancient canal had been shut up. The distance between the Kin k'ou and the village of Kao-li chuang, where the canal had to reach the 御河 *Yü ho* (Imperial canal), he reckoned 120 *li*.[93] This proposition was discussed in the council of ministers and many objections were made. One of them recalled to mind the fact, that in the year 1298, owing to great inundations caused by the Hun ho and the consequent danger to the capital, the canal had been shut up. But notwithstanding these objections the emperor ordered the digging of the projected canal to be executed; the Kin k'ou was opened and the whole work finished in four months. The result was unsatisfactory however; for the water deposited much mud and the boats could not go. At other times inundations caused mischief."

The authenticity of the ancient Chinese statements above translated, regarding the diversion of a part of the water of the *Hun ho* to the capital of the Kin in the 12th century, can be easily proved by local observation. A few weeks ago I undertook, in company with my friend Dr. von Moellendorff, to search for the traces of this channel. Although only guided by the ancient description, we had no difficulty in finding the bed, and also the villages mentioned in the ancient accounts; for they have preserved the same names up to this time.

At a distance of about 40 *li*, straight west of the *P'ing-tse men* (one of the western gates of the capital), just at the place where the Hun ho emerges from the mountains into the plain, there is on the left bank of the river, an isolated hill 470 English feet high, which is known under the name of 石景山 *Shi-king shan*. It is crowned by an ancient monastery, and picturesque ruins are scattered about on its slopes, dating partly from the time of the Kin; but for the greater part the construction of these palace buildings is attributed to the Ming emperors. The western side of the Shi-king shan forms a steep precipice down to the Hun ho. To the north, the hill is separated by a deep depression from the last spur of the mountain chain, following the left bank of the river. This passage, about half a *li* broad, is not more than 40 or 50 feet above the level of the Hun ho. It is still

---

93. Evidently the principal object in view was to introduce a large quantity of water into the Transport canal.

called by its ancient name 金口 *Kin k'ou* (Golden defile). The village 麻峪 *Ma-yü*, mentioned by the ancient authors as the starting point of the channel, lies near the western entrance of it, on the left bank of the river. It was easy for us to detect here the dried-up bed of the channel, passing through the Kin k'ou, and shut up by a solid dike just as is reported in the ancient accounts. One of the roads leading from Peking to the coal mines in the Western mountains, passes over this dike. Even the safety channel, dug in 1265, which turned around the Hun ho to the south-west to prevent the danger which might arise to the capital from sudden freshets (see above), still exists. (Compare map IV.)

We had not the slightest difficulty in pursuing the course of the ancient Hun-ho channel, which is known to the people under the name of 金口河 *Kin-k'ou ho* (river from the Kin k'ou), from Kin k'ou down to the western precincts of Peking. The dry bed of the channel, now used almost throughout its whole extent for agricultural purposes, is lined by solid embankments from 15 to 20 feet high. It has a width of about 120 English feet, and has not been dug in a straight line, but crosses the plain in numerous windings. The reason of this disposition is easily understood. The ancient engineers tried by this way to diminish the rapid current; for Kin k'ou is according to ancient measurements 140 feet higher than Peking. To introduce the water of the Hun ho into the dry bed again would present no difficulty.

After quitting Kin k'ou, the channel passes south of the large village of 北辛莊 *Pei-sin an*, and pursuing its course to the east, we meet on its northern bank the village of 陽家莊 *Yang-kia chuang* (village of the Yang family). I have little doubt, that this is the same place mentioned in the ancient records under the name of 上陽村 *Shang yang-t'sun* (upper village of Yang) as having been damaged in A.D. 1175, by an inundation caused by the waters of the Hun-ho channel (see above). Thence the channel runs eastward, and passes between the group of hills rising in the western Peking plain, and known under the name of 八寶山 *Pa-pao shan* (on one of the hills there is a monastery of this name). The course of the channel lies one *li* and more south of the large village of 田村 *T'ien-ts'un*, well known to all Europeans in Peking; for it is situated on the road to the temples of 八大處 *Pa-ta-ch'u*, the summer residence of the British Legation. Further on, the channel passes near the lake of *Wang-hai-lou* (or *Tiao-yü-t'ai*), mentioned above, but does not communicate with it. Perhaps they were in connection in ancient times. The lake in its present form is a creation of the emperor Kien-lung in the last century; but as I have stated above, at the time of the Kin dynasty there was a lake and a pleasure ground at the same place.

The course of the ancient channel from the last-named place downward requires further investigation; for its traces become uncertain, owing to numerous ravines occurring in the country, and caused by the cart-roads converging towards the capital. Besides this, numerous villages and farms have effaced the traces of the channel. Nevertheless I have little doubt that from Wang-hai-lou it turned (one branch at least) to the south-east, and went to the marsh called *Lien-hua ch'i*, "Lotus pond" (see above). There is near this marsh a stone bridge (evidently not of very ancient date) over the ravine, which I suppose to have been the bed of the Hun-ho channel. As I have shown in another chapter of this paper, the north-western corner of the ancient Kin capital must have been situated near this place. We have seen also, that according to the ancient authors, the Hun-ho channel had been conducted into the northern moat of that capital.

I did not pursue my investigations regarding the bed of the ancient channel in its course east of Peking. The Chinese annals record, that it had been led into the river *Pai ho* at a place south of T'ung chou called *Kao-li chuang* (see above).

At the time Marco Polo was in Peking the Hun-ho channel was supplied with water; for as has been stated above, Coubilaï khan gave orders to open the ancient channel dug by the Kin. It was only in 1298 (after Polo's departure) that it was shut up again.

M. Polo states (l.c. vol. i, p. 331), that the Great Kaan caused Kambaluc to be built close beside the old city (of the Kin) with only a river between them. I do not think that the traveller could have meant the Hun-ho channel. There is a strong probability that he speaks of the 文明河 *Wen-ming ho*, a river which according to the ancient descriptions ran near the southern wall of the Mongol capital.

The *Ch'un ming meng yü lu* (cf. *Ji hia*, chap. lv, fol. 2), published under the Ming dynasty, states:—"The river 三里河 *San-li ho* was called 文明河 *Wen-ming ho* in the time of the Yüan. It was used for the transport of corn, and was in connection with the (principal) Transport canal." At the time the author wrote (first half of the 17th century) an ancient iron lock could still be seen in the river.

Further particulars regarding the *San-li ho* may be found in the *Ji hia*, chap. lv, fol. 3. I will not translate these accounts, but confine myself to mentioning that traces of a river bed can still be found in the Chinese city, north of the temples of Heaven and of Agriculture. The authors of the Ming mention the *San-li ho* or *Wen-ming ho* south of the southern wall of the capital. I may observe, that one of the southern gates of the Mongol capital was called *Wen-ming men*. Probably the name was drawn from the name of the river.

The name of *San-li ho* is now applied only to the river which issues from the lake of Wang-hai-lou and discharges into the moat of Peking at the south-western corner of the Tartar city (see map IV; and *Ji hia*, chap. xcv, fol. 7).

We may conclude, that in ancient times the river passed between Khanbaligh and the Kin capital, and then took a south-eastern direction.

>The preceding four maps are intended to render more intelligible the ancient accounts regarding the Chinese capital.
>
>No. I. represents modern Peking and the position of the ancient ramparts found in its neighborhood. On this map only such names are marked as appear in my article; and I have indicated none of the ancient names. On the square to the left, the reader will find the Chinese names of the eleven gates of the Mongol capital, as enumerated by ancient authors.
>
>No. II. represents the palace and the palace grounds of the present dynasty.
>
>In No. III. I have attempted to draw up a plan of the Mongol palaces, according to the Chinese descriptions; but these descriptions not being always very explicit, I have been obliged in some cases to fill in. The reader, in comparing the map with the descriptions however, will easily understand what I have presumed to add.
>
>No. IV. represents the environs of Peking, and shows especially the watercourses in the Peking plain in our day.

THE BRIDGE *LU-KOU K'IAO* AND THE *HUN HO* OR *SANG-KAN* RIVER, WITH THE ROAD TO SHANG-TU.

About seven English miles south-west of Peking is the celebrated stone bridge 盧溝橋 *Lu-kou k'iao*, one of the eight wonders of the capital (see note 20), leading over the *Hun ho*.[94] All the great roads from the provinces leading to the capital pass by this bridge. It is the only stone bridge spanning the Hun ho; and as the water of this river in the rainy season often rises considerably, the bridge is of the greatest importance for the communication. A splendid road, paved with large square stones has been constructed from the Chang-yi men towards the bridge, but does not reach it. Several *li* before arriving at the river it finishes with a beautiful triumphal arch or gateway, erected by the emperor Kien-lung in the last century. The traveller meets on this road, at all seasons of the year, large caravans of camels laden with coals carried from the Western mountains. Before arriving at the bridge the small walled city of 拱極城 *Kung-ki cheng* is passed. This was founded in the first half of the 17th century (*Ji hia*, chap. xcii, fol. 13). The people generally call it 肥城 *Fei ch'eng*.

Marco Polo in his narrative, devotes a chapter to the Lu-kou k'iao (Yule, l. c. vol. ii, p. 1). The bridge has often been spoken of by the commentators of the great traveller; and besides some Chinese accounts of the bridge known in Europe from translations, it has repeated-

---

[94]. The Chinese estimate the distance between the Chang-yi gate and the bridge generally at 25 *li*; the Chinese *Merchant's Guide* has 30 *li*; but both figures are too high, the distance not being more than 21 *li*.

ly been mentioned by European travellers of past centuries. But as these accounts are not always in accordance, I undertook a short time ago to repair to the bridge with the view of investigating it, and now give the following description. The bridge is 350 ordinary paces long and 18 broad. It is built of sandstone, and has on either side a stone balustrade of square columns, about 4 feet high, 140 on each side, each crowned by a sculptured lion over a foot high. Beside these there are a number of smaller lions placed irregularly on the necks, behind the legs, under the feet, or on the back of the larger ones.[95] The space between the columns is closed by stone slabs. Four sculptured stone elephants lean with their foreheads against the edge of the balustrades. The bridge is supported by eleven arches.[96] At each end of the bridge two pavilions with yellow roofs have been built, all with large marble tablets in them; two with inscriptions made by order of the emperor Kang-hi (1662-1723); and two with inscriptions of the time of Ki'en-lung (1736-1796). On these tablets the history of the bridge is recorded. Compare also *Ji hia*, chaps. xcii and xciii. Previous to the 13th century there were only wooden bridges over the Hun ho. A Chinese traveller, who went from the south to Peking in 1123,[97] gives the following statement:—

"We left *Liang-hiang hien* (this city still bears the same name) and after 30 *li* arrived at the *Lu-kou* river (the same as the Hun ho). It runs very rapidly; and in time of low water temporary bridges are laid over it (as now in winter time). Some years ago the 都水監 *Tu-shui-kien* (Inspector of the Water conveyances) made a floating bridge (浮橋) over the river, and fixed it to both banks."

In another work, quoted in the *Ji hia*, chap. civ, fol. 5, the destruction of the bridge by fire, in the same year, 1123, is recorded.

A stone bridge over the Hun ho was first built at the end of the 12th century by order of the Kin emperor *Ming-ch'ang*. The work was finished in five years, 1189-1192.

Under the succeeding dynasties the bridge has repeatedly been damaged by floods, and its restoration is frequently recorded in Chinese annals. But judging from the Chinese statements, it seems never to have been entirely destroyed; for the Chinese authors always speak merely of repairs.

M. Polo, who saw the bridge a hundred years after it had been built, describes it in the following terms (Yule, l. c. vol. ii, pp. 1, 2):—

"When you leave the City of Combaluc and have ridden ten

---

95. The Chinese say no one has ever succeeded in counting the lions on the bridge; and indeed it is difficult to count all the small lions.
96. Dr. Lockhart (see Yule, l. c., vol. ii, p. 4), counted nine arches. He is also right, for he counts only the waterways, not the arches resting upon the banks of the river.
97. 許奉使行程錄. See my *Notes on Chinese Mediæval Travellers*, p. 122.

miles, you come to a very large river which is called PULISANGHIN, and flows into the ocean, so that merchants with their merchandize ascend it from the sea. Over this River there is a very fine stone bridge, so fine indeed that it has very few equals. The fashion of it is this: it is 300 paces in length, and it must have a good eight paces of width, for ten mounted men can ride across it abreast. It has 24 arches and as many water-mills, and 'tis all of very fine marble, well built and firmly founded. Along the top of the bridge there is on either side a parapet of marble slabs and columns, made in this way. At the beginning of the bridge there is a marble column, and under it a marble lion, so that the column stands upon the lion's loins, whilst on the top of the column there is a second marble lion, both being of great size and beautifully executed sculpture. At the distance of a pace from this column there is another precisely the same, also with its two lions, and the space between them is closed with slabs of grey marble to prevent people from falling over into the water. And thus the columns run from space to space along either side of the bridge."

Comparing M. Polo's account of the bridge with the description of it I have given above from my own observation, we may conclude that the ancient bridge was longer than the present; for M. Polo's paces are geometrical paces,—1 pace = 5 feet (see Yule, l. c. vol. ii, p. 472). The bridge Polo saw had 24 arches, and large lions crowned the columns. It seems that at the place where the present bridge stands, the banks of the river, which is of considerable breadth have been artificially elevated and advanced from both sides in order to narrow the bed.

I have not been able to find a Chinese description of the Lu-kou bridge by an author contemporary with M. Polo. The most ancient Chinese description existing seems to be that found in the *Ch'ang an k'o hua* (end of the 16th cent.) chap, iv, fol. 14. There it is stated, that the Lu-kou k'iao is more than 200 *pu* (1000 feet) long, and that it has a stone balustrade on the left and on the right. On the balustrade there are several hundred sculptured lions (on either side); but it is impossible to count them. Whoever tries to do so is sure to make a mistake.

I cannot say whether this author speaks of Polo's bridge. As I have stated above, the Chinese authors do not record, that the bridge built in the 12th century has ever been entirely destroyed and rebuilt. The Jesuits however, who resided at Peking in the 17th century, report that the whole bridge fell down during their sojourn in the capital. I may quote here a book of great rarity to which I have access, where the destruction of the bridge is mentioned with some particulars: *Compendiosa narratione dello stato della Missione Cinese, cominciado dall anno* 1581 *fino al* 1669. *Offerta in Roma, &c. dal P. Prospero Intorcetta della Compagnia di Giesu, Missionario e. Procuratore della Cina.* In

Roma per Fr. Fizzoni, 1672. In this book, p. 65, is the following record:—"Nel medesimo giorno 25 di Luglio 1668 rouinarono due degli archi di quel famoso ponte di Pekino, la di cui longitudine passa un terzo di un miglio, opera Reale di bianchissima pietra, molto larga, e di smisurata altezza, tanto bella alla vista per l'artificio e Mæsta, che pareva d'essere nuovamête fabricata, havendo di già compiti mille anni d'antichità. Fini doppo di rovinare tutta in Augusto, come appresso si dira."

Again on page 73:—"Finalmente in questo giorno medesimo fini di rovinare quel famoso Ponte, non molto distante dalle muraglie di Pekino, che accenai di sopra, degno veramente d'essere annoverato tra miracoli del mondo. Si ritrovò nelle rovine una grâ pietra, ch' hauea scolpiti in se 4. versi di carratteri Cinese, quali si vedono qui sotto pronūciati alla Cinese.

16	xao	11	xe	6	ya	1	çie
17	çin	12	leao	7	tao	2	leam
18	si	13	nan	8	lo	3	quam
19	xan	14	lai	9	keu	4	che
20	mui	15	mi	10	kiao	5	quo

"Il senso litterale delli sudetti versi e questo:—*Passato* che sarà il *carro* di *çie leam quam* (non s'ha potuto sapere il senso di quelle tre lettere, çie leam quam: pare che dinotino un nome proprio di quell' huomo, ò di quella cosa, che doveva passare nel carro) rovinera questo *ponte* chiamato Lo keu: e si *finirà* di *mangiare* il *riso* che *viene* alla corte di *Pekino* dalle parti *Australi*: si finirà pure di *abbruciare* il *carbone* che viene alla corte dalli monti *occidentali*: fin qui il senso de versi."[98]

Magaillans, quoted by Yule (l. c. vol. ii, pp. 3, 4, gives the 17th Aug. 1688 as the date of the destruction of the bridge.[99] But Intorcetta's date (1668) agrees well with the Chinese accounts. On one of the abovementioned tablets erected near the bridge, it is recorded, that the bridge had been repaired in 1669 by order of the emperor Kang-hi. I observe that in the inscription the character 修 (to repair) is used. Thus the bridge may not have been entirely thrown down as Intorcetta states. However I leave it to the reader to decide with respect to the conflicting accounts of western and eastern authors.

---

[98]. I shall attempt to restore the Chinese characters of the inscription Intorcetta saw, according to his indications. I do not think, that the first three characters denoted the name of a man or a thing as Intorcetta asserts.

16	燒	11	食	6	壓	1	藉
17	盡	12	了	7	倒	2	糧
18	西	13	南	8	盧	3	官
19	山	14	來	9	溝	4	車
20	煤	15	米	10	橋	5	過

[99]. I have not seen the original. Perhaps there is a misprint in Col. Yule's note.

The name *Pulisanghin* used by M. Polo to designate the river over which the bridge stood, has been quite satisfactorily explained by the commentators of M. Polo. Pul in Persian means "a bridge," and by *Sanghin* Polo renders the Chinese 桑乾 *Sang-kan*, by which name the river Hun ho is already mentioned in the 6th century of our era (*Ji hia*, chap. xcii, fol. 5). 渾河 *Hun ho* is also an ancient name; and the same river in ancient books is often called 盧溝河 *Lu-kou* river also. All these names are in use up to the present time; but on modern Chinese maps, only the upper part of the river is termed *Sang-kan ho*, whilst south of the inner Great wall, and in the plain, the name of *Hun ho* is applied to it. *Hun ho* means "Muddy river," and the term is quite suitable. In the last century the emperor K'ien-lung ordered the Hun ho to be named 永定河 *Yung-ting ho*, a name found on modern maps, but the people always call it *Hun ho*.

I may observe that the name *Sanghin* for the river in question is met also in Rashid-eddin's description of Khanbaligh and its environs (Yule's *Cathay*, vol. ii, p. 260). The Persian historiographer states:—
"The Kaan's intention was to build a palace like that of *Daidu* at *Kaiminfu* (K'ai-ping fu or Shang-tu) which is at a distance of fifty parasangs, and to reside there. There are three roads to that place from the winter residence. The first, reserved for hunting matches, is allowed to be used only by ambassadors. The second road passes by the city of *Chúchú*, following the banks of the *Sanghin* river, where you see great plenty of grapes and other kinds of fruit. Near the city just named there is another called SEMALI, most of the inhabitants of which are natives of Samarkand, and have planted a number of gardens in the Samarkand. style. The third road takes the direction of the pass of *Siking* (other readings:—*Sengking*,—*Sengling*), and after traversing this you find only prairies and plains abounding in game until you reach the city of Kaiminfu, where the summer palace is. Formerly the court used to pass the summer in the vicinty of *Chúchú*, but afterwards the neighborhood of Kaiminfu was preferred, and on the eastern side of that city a *karsi* or palace was built called *Langtin*, after a plan which the Kaan had seen in a dream, and retained in his memory (according to D'Ohsson's translation,* the Kaan abandoned the palace in consequence of a dream)."

I am indebted to Archimandrite Palladius for the communication of a Chinese pamphlet (in manuscript) 元上都驛程考 *Yüan shang tu yi ch'eng k'ao*, "Researches on the stations on the roads leading from the Mongol capital to *Shang tu* (the summer residence of the Mongol emperors)," which enables me to elucidate Raschid's statements regarding the same roads, by means of contemporary Chinese documents. The pamphlet in question has been compiled by a learned Chinese of our days, from works written in the Mongol times. The author quotes especially the

well-known writer 周伯琦 *Ch'ou Po-k'i*, who lived in the first half of the
14th century.[100] The *Yüan shang tu yi ch'eng k'ao* has never been published. Palladius received his manuscript copy from the author, whom
he knew personally. Most of the matter however, brought together in
this pamphlet, and arranged systematically, can be found also in the
承德府志 *Cheng te fu chi*, a geographical and historical description of
the department of Ch'eng-te fu (or *Jehol*). In chap, lx, fol. 26-37, the
itineraries of four Chinese travellers of the 13th and 14th centuries, from
Peking to *Shang-tu* and *Caracorum* are reprinted.[101] Many interesting
ancient accounts on the same subject are also collected in the 口北三
廳志 *K'ou pei san t'ing chi*, a historical and geographical description
of the land north of the Great wall, belonging to the jurisdiction of
Chang-kia-k'ou (*Kalgan*), *Tu-shi-k'ou* and *Dolonnor*, published in 1758
in 16 books, with a map appended. Compare also the 宣化府志 *Süan
hua fu chi*, a geographical and historical description of the department
of *Süan hua fu*, published in 1743, in 42 books; a number of detailed
maps being appended to the work. As to the modern names of places,
which I am obliged to quote in the following investigations, I beg the
reader to refer also to the large Chinese map of the imperial dominions
大清一統輿圖 *Ta ts'ing yi t'ung yü t'u*, published in *Wu-chang fu*, by the
governor of the province of Hupei in 1863, and to *M. C. Wæber's* excellent
map of the province of Chili, published in Russian at St. Petersburg
in 1871. This latter is the only detailed European map for this part
of China. Some years ago my friend *Dr. Bushell* visited the ruins of
Shang-tu, and described the result of his investigations in two interesting
papers read before the Royal Geographical Society, and the Royal Asiatic
Society. One of these papers is accompanied by a very good map, which
will also be serviceable in following my remarks. The accompanying
sketch map referring to the routes to Shangtu, has only modern names
of places.

---

100. See his biography in the *Yüan shi*, chap. clxxxvii.
101. 周伯琦扈從北行前記
　　　周伯琦扈從北行後記
　　　張德輝嶺北紀行
　　　王輝中堂事紀

MAP V.

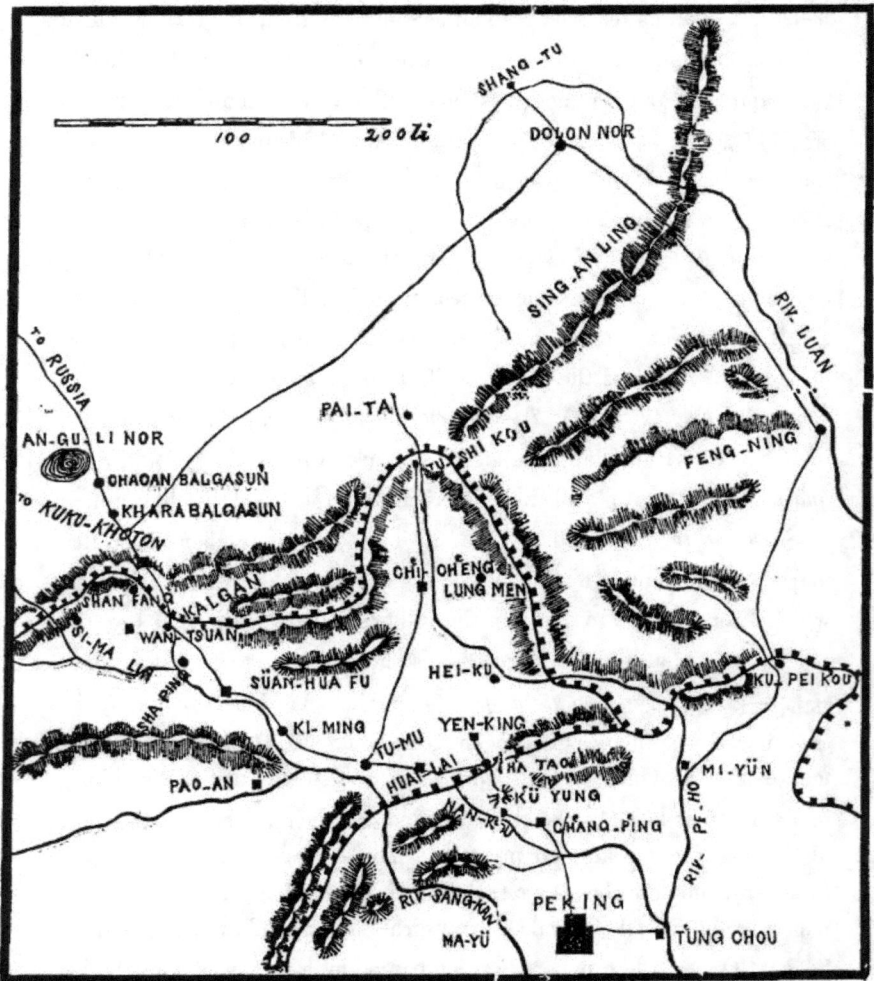

According to the authors of the Mongol dynasty, there were indeed, as Rashid-eddin states, *three roads* in use between *Tai-tu* (Khanbaligh) and the summer residence *Shang-tu*. The same roads still exist, and for the greater part pass by the same places as mentioned on them six hundred years ago.

The first of these roads, the shortest of all,—which went from the Mongol capital to the summer residence in a nearly straight direction and is estimated it seems, at 750 *li* by the ancient Chinese authors,—passed by the defile of 居庸 Kü-yung (Nan-k'ou pass of Europeans), which is situated to the north-west of Peking (see maps IV and V). As may be concluded from the stations enumerated in the ancient itinerary, this road went from the Nan-k'ou pass straight northward to the gate 獨石口 Tu-shi-k'ou (of the Great wall). This name, however, does not appear in the itinerary. It seems that it was not in use at the time of the Mongols. There were eighteen 納鉢 na-bo,[102] or imperial stations, on this road; so that the distance between any two stations was 42 li on an average. I shall in what follows, quote from the ancient itinerary such names of stations only, as can be identified with places marked on modern maps.

After issuing from the Kü-yung defile the road went to the city of 縉山縣 Tsin-shan hien, which is, according to the Chinese geographical dictionary Li tai ti li chi, the same as the present 延慶州 Yen-king chou, north of the defile.

Further on, the station 黑谷 Hei-ku (Black valley) is mentioned. Now there is a military post 黑谷所 Hei-ku su, north-east of Yen-king chow. See the corresponding map in the Süan hua fu chi.

Then the ancient way led through the 龍門 Lung-men (Dragon's gate). A military post of this name is marked on the same map east of the city of 赤城 Ch'i-ch'eng. This city, through which the road to Tu-shi-k'ou now passes, did not exist at the time of the Yüan. It was founded by the Ming.

I cannot identify the next five stations. The sixth is called 白塔兒 Pai-t'a-r (White tower). A place of this name is marked on the modern map of the Great wall, as found in the Süan hua fu chi, north of Tu-shi-k'ou.

Four stations after leaving Pai-t'a-r, the lake 察罕腦兒 Ch'a-han nao-r (Chagan nor "White lake") was reached. This lake was at a distance of three days journey (seven stations) from Shang-tu. The second station from Shang-tu, was the city of 桓州 Huan-chou. When the Mongol emperors went to Shang-tu for the summer, they followed the straight road, and used to return in autumn by the western road.

This straight road to Shang-tu was probably Rashid-eddin's "first,

---

102. According to Archimandrite Palladius' investigations, nabo is a K'itan word, and has the same meaning as the Chinese 行宮 hing-kung, or "imperial travelling palace (station)." On all the roads where the emperor used to travel, such small palaces had been erected for his convenience; and it is the same even now. Numerous travelling palaces or hing-kung, or their ruins, belonging to the time of Kang-hi or K'ien-lung, are to be found in the province of Chili. In my "Notes on Chinese Mediæval Travellers," p. 25, I translated hing-kung,—which term had been identified by the traveller Ch'ang-ch'un with the Mongol ordo,—by "moveable palace." I would observe, that this translation is correct only with respect to Tchinguiz khan's time, for the great conqueror lived in tents. It was his successor Ogotaï, who first built palaces.

reserved for hunting matches,—allowed to be used only by ambassadors."

Let me inquire into the itinerary of the second road to Shang-tu as given by the ancient Chinese authors. This,—known under the name of "western road,"—also passed through the *Kü-yung* defile, and then branched off westward from the first described straight road. At the northern issue of the defile there is now the little town of 岔道 *Ch'a-tao*. This name means "road bifurcation;" for at this place even now the road divides; one branch leading to *Yen-king chou*, the other to *Süan-hua fu* and *Kalgan*. Up to Süan-hua fu, the modern road is the same as that described as the western road by the ancient authors. The western road measured 1095 *li* between the winter and summer residences.[103] Twenty-four stations had been established on it. The stations 懷來縣 *Huai-lai hien*, 榆林 *Yü-lin*, 狼山 *Lang-shan*, 統幕 *T'ung-mu*,[104] and 雞鳴山 *Ki-ming shan*, mentioned in the ancient itinerary, have still the same names, and all lie on the great highway to *Süan-hua fu*. This latter place is called 順寧府 *Shun-ning fu* in the itinerary.[105] Beyond Süan-hua fu, the modern road (by which Dr. Bushell proceeded to Shang-tu) leads straight to Kalgan (or 張家口 *Chang-kia-k'ou*), whilst the ancient road seems to have followed the 洋河 *Yang ho* upwards; for the next station mentioned in the itinerary is 沙嶺 *Sha-ling*, which on modern Chinese maps is marked on the bank of this river, west of the Kalgan road.[106]

The next station was 得勝口 *Te-sheng-k'ou*. The itinerary speaks of a palace here with flower gardens, planted also with various kinds of fruit trees. This name is not marked on modern maps, but it must have been situated west of modern Kalgan.

The next station was on the top of the pass called 野狐嶺 *Ye-hu ling*.[107]

---

103. Dr. Bushell, who proceeded from Peking to Shang-tu, passing through Süan-hua fu and Kalgan, estimates the distance at only 950 *li*. But as we shall see, the ancient road went, not through Kalgan, but made a turn to the west. Rashid-eddin states that Shang-tu is distant from Khanbaligh 50 *parasangs*. According to D'Herbelot (*Bibliothèque Orientale*, p. 504, article "Khathouat"), an (ancient) parasang was equal to 36,000 feet. As the Chinese *li* has 1800 feet, one parasang = about 20 *li*, and 50 parasangs = about 1000 *li*. Thus Rashid's statement is in accordance with the Chinese. M. Polo states, l. c. vol. i, p. 389, that Cambaluc is distant from Shang-tu ten days journey. He means probably the direct road with eighteen imperial stations; for he speaks of the way followed by the khan's foot-runners.

104. *T'ung-mu* on modern Chinese maps is written 土木 *T'u-mu*. It is a little town.

105. The present departmental town of 宣化府 *Süan-hua fu*, under the Kin dynasty was called 宣德州 *Süan-te chou*. After it had been taken by the Mongols, the name was changed into 宣寧府 *Süan-ning fu*. In 1263 the ancient name of *Süan-te* was again adopted (*Süan-te fu*), but in 1266 changed again into 順寧府 *Shun-ning fu* (cf. *Yi t'ung chi*, the great geography of China). Marco Polo calls Süan-hua fu, *Sindachau*, which name is intended for Süan-te chou as Col. Yule first pointed out.

106. Compare the corresponding map in the *Süan hua fu chi* and Wæber's map.

107. *Ye-hu ling*, according to the *K'ou pei san t'ing chi*, chap. ii, fol. 6, is situated at a

ON PEKING AND ITS ENVIRONS.   59

The next station, 30 *li* to the north, was the departmental city of 興和路 *Hing-ho lu*.[108]

The seventh station after leaving *Hing-ho lu*, was on the lake *Ch'a-han nao-r* (Chagan nor) already mentioned. Here the direct road and the western road united.[109]

---

distance of 5 *li* north of the 膳房堡口 *Shan-fang-p'u k'ou*. The latter is the name of one of the gates in the Great wall, next to the west after the gate of Kalgan. Compare the map in the *K'ou pei, etc. Ch'ang-ch'un*, on his journey from Peking to Mongolia in 1221, passed by the Ye-hu ling defile (See my *Notes on Chinese Mediæval Travellers*, p. 19). Another Chinese traveller, *Chang Te-hui*, proceeding about the middle of the 13th century from Peking to Caracorum, mentions his passing through the gate of *Te-sheng k'ou*, (see above;—this seems to be the same as the modern *Shan-fang-p'u k'ou*), after which he reached the 扼狐嶺 *O-hu ling*. *Ling*, as is known, in Chinese means "a pass" and also "a ridge of a mountain;" *ye-hu* or *ô-hu* represents probably a Mongol word. *Yeke* = "big."

108. *Hing-ho lu* is the present *Khara-balgasun* (Black city) about 30 English miles north west of Kalgan, situated on the caravan road to Russia, and also the same as 撫州 *Fu chou* mentioned in Ch'ang-ch'un's itinerary (*Notes on Chinese Mediæval Travellers*, p. 19). *Fu chou* was a very important place under the *Kin* dynasty in the 12th century, as well as in the beginning of the Mongol era. The original name was changed in 1262 into 隆興路 *Lung-hing lu* (*lu* = "departmental city" in the Mongol time), and subsequently into *Hing-ho lu*. The *Kin* emperors had a palace there (*Kin shi*,—geographical part), and according to the *Yüan shi* (annals, sub anno 1263) a *hing-kung* or "imperial travelling palace" was built at this place. In the *Yüan shi* (annals, sub anno 1293), it is recorded, that at Hing-ho lu a manufactory for the equipment of the troops (軍器人匠局) was established. I quote this statement, for Marco Polo (l. c., vol. i, p. 251) reports the same with respect to *Sindacku* (Süan-hua fu),—"they carry on a great many crafts such as provide for the equipment of the Emperor's troops." It results from the date given by the Chinese authors, that the manufactory in Hing-ho lu was established only after M. Polo had left China.

109. The lake of *Chagan nor* (White lake) is mentioned also by M. Polo (l. c. vol. i, p. 260) on his road from Süan-hua fu to Shang-tu. He places it, just as the ancient Chinese authors do (*K'ou pei san etc*, chap. ii, fol. 10), midway between the two cities, i. e. at a distance of three days from Shang-tu and the same distance from Süan-hua fu. One of the travellers quoted in the *Ch'eng te fu chi* (l. c.) took five days between Süan-hua fu and Ch'agan nor, travelling evidently very slowly. Dr. Bushell in his pamphlet quoted above, identifies M. Polo's Chagan nor with *Chagan-balgasun*, about 8 English miles north-west of *Khara-balgasun*. Before him the same identification had been made by Ritter (*Asien*, vol. i, p. 123), and Prof. Semionoff (Russian translation of Ritter, vol. i, p. 338), and Col. Yule also adopts this view, which however is in contradiction with the Chinese authors of the Mongol period, whilst the Chinese statements are in accordance with M. Polo. *Chagan-balgasun* (White city) is the name applied by the Mongols of our days to the ruins of an ancient city, which according to A. Palladius' investigations, based on local observation, must be identified with ancient 昌州 *Ch'ang chou*, built by the Kin in the 12th century (*cf. Notes on Chinese Mediæval Travellers*, p. 20, note 22). Chagan-balgasun had already been mentioned before Palladius, in 1819 by *Timkowsky* (Russian edition, vol. iii, p. 35). According to the latter, these ruins are found a little to the south-east of the lake *Angulinor*, identified by Ritter and others with M. Polo's Chagan nor. Dr. Bushell saw the ruins of Chagan-balgasun only from afar, at a distance of 45 *li*, and was told by the people (it seems) that the adjoining lake is called *Chagan nor*. I can find no corroboration in Chinese works for the Anguli nor being named also Chagan nor, and may observe that the latter is a very common name for lakes in Mongolia, occurring frequently on the Chinese maps of that country; but I have not been able to make out a lake of this name marked in the regions between Khara-balgasun and Shang-tu. This part of Mongolia, as is known, abounds in lakes. The *K'ou pei san etc.*, describes all the principal lakes outside the Great wall, comparing ancient statements regarding them with modern accounts; but as to the Chagan nor in question, it is mentioned only by quotations drawn from ancient authors, and nothing is said about its position now. According to the Chinese annals, Coubilai khan had built a palace near this lake, in 1280. M. Polo speaks also of this palace. My objections to the view, that

I have little doubt, that this western road to Shang-tu, described in ancient Chinese works, is identical with the second road of Rashid, following the banks of the river *Sanghin*, passing near the city of *Semali*, and through the city of *Chúchú*. The road from Peking to Süanhua fu proceeds indeed for a long distance in the valley of the river *Sang-kan* (see above), and the 洋河 *Yang-ho*, which is an affluent of the latter. We have seen, that in the Mongol times the way to Shang-tu went, not through Kalgan as it does now, but lay more to the west. About twenty English miles west of Kalgan there is a place called 洗馬林 *Si-ma lin*, marked on most of the Chinese maps, and on Wæber's map, which I presume to be Rashid's *Semali*. I am strengthened in my view by the fact, that a place of a similar name is mentioned in the history of the Mongol dynasty.

In the *Yüan-shi*, chap. clxiv, biography of *Kuo Shou-king* (see note 80), it is stated, that in the year 1291 two propositions were laid before the emperor. The first was to establish a water conveyance between 永平 *Yung-p'ing* (now Yung-p'ing fu in the north-eastern part of the province of Chili) and *Shang-tu* on the river 灤 *Luan* (or *Shang-tu gol*) but the boats would have had to be drawn over the mountains.[110] The second project was to render navigable the *Lu-kou* river (*Hun-ho* or *Sang-kan*;—see above) from *Ma-yü* (a village already mentioned, on the Hun-ho, west of Peking, where the river emerges into the plain) upwards to 尋麻林 *Sin-ma lin*. The emperor ordered Kuo Shou-king to investigate the matter by local observation. Both projects were found to be impracticable.[111]

Chagan nor of the Mongol period is to be identified with the *Anguli nor* near Chagan-balgasun, is based on the ancient Chinese statements, that the straight road from Peking to Shang-tu passed by Chagan nor, and that this lake is stated to be situated midway between Shang-tu and Süan-hua fu, when proceeding by the western road. I think, therefore, its position must be looked for a considerable distance north-east of Chagan-balgasun; for this latter place is distant from Shang-tu twice as much as from Süan-hua fu. Besides these arguments, I can give more positive indications drawn from ancient sources, supporting my view regarding the position of M. Polo's Chagan nor. In the *Kin shi*, chap. xxiv, geographical section, I find that near the city of 柔遠縣 *Jou-yüan hien* belonging to *Fu chou* (Khara-balgasun), is the lake 昂吉里 *Ang-gi-li*, called also 鴛鴦 *Yüan-yang* lake. The explanatory dictionary for the *Kin shi* informs us, that *angir*, represented by the Chinese sounds *ang-gi-li*, means " a wild duck" in Mongol (probably also in the language of the Liao or Kin ; *angir* has the same meaning in Manchu). The Chinese *yüan-yang* is applied to the beautiful " mandarin duck (*anas galericulata*)," found all over Mongolia and China. Yüan-yang is up to our days the Chinese name of the lake marked on Chinese and European maps as Anguli nor (*cf.* *Yi t'ung chi*), and is a literal translation of that original Mongol name, somewhat corrupted, on modern Chinese maps (昂古立騰兒 *An-gu-li nao-r*). In one of the ancient Chinese itineraries quoted above, a statement is found that the lake *Yüan-yang* is more than 100 *li* distant from the Changan nor, and that numerous other lakes, abounding in water-fowl, are seen on this tract. This position assigned to Chagan nor (100 *li* to the north-east of the Anguli nor is to be understood) would bring it about midway between Süan-hua fu and Shang-tu.

110. 言灤河自永平挽舟踰山而上可至開平.
111. As to the *Luan* river however, it was made navigable in Coubilai's time, **as the same**

Thus Rashid's *Semali* can be identified. Rashid speaks of the splendid gardens and orchards at this place. The ancient Chinese itineraries mention imperial orchards and flower gardens near *Te-sheng k'ou* (see above), which place must have been near the present *Si-ma lin*. Rashid states further that at Semali people of Samarcand were settled. Even in our days a great number of Mohammedans live in the cities and villages between Peking and Kalgan, and especially towards the latter place. They are, in all probability, descendants of those Mohammedans spoken of by M. Polo as inhabitants of the towns and villages he passed through before arriving at Süan-hua fu, and mentioned by Rashid as settled in the same region.

The identification of the city of *Chúchú*, in the vicinity of Semali according to Rashid, and situated on the road to Shang-tu presents some difficulties. The commentators of Rashid, probably seduced by the similarity of sounds, do not hesitate in identifying Chúchú with 涿州 *Cho chou*.[112] But this city is situated 130 *li* south-west of Peking, while Shang-tu lies straight to the north of the capital. I have no doubt that Chúchú is a clerical error in the Persian manuscripts. Perhaps it ought to be read *Fuchu* and the city of *Fu chou* (Kharabalgasun;—see note 108) is to be understood. We have seen that this city was an important place in the time of the Kin. The emperors of that dynasty had a palace there according to the Chinese annals. In the *Yüan shi*, chap. iv, annals of *Coubilaï khan*, at the beginning, we find some additional corroborations of the view, that Rashid's *Chúchú* may be identified with ancient *Fu chou*. It is stated there, that in 1252, when Coubilaï was still heir-apparent, he established his *ordo* between 桓州 *Huan chou* (see above) and 撫州 *Fu chou*. In 1254, after returning from the expedition to Yünnan, he dwelt at first at the same place, and then transferred his residence to *Fu chou*. In 1255 his encampment was again between *Huan chou* and *Fu chou*. In 1256, in spring, a Buddhist priest was ordered to look out by divination for a prosperous place, east of *Huan chou* and north of the 灤 *Luan* (*Shang-tu gol*;—see notes 110, 111) suitable for the foundation of a city, which (afterwards) was called 開平 *K'ai-p'ing*. Coubilaï spent the winter of the same year in the country of 哈剌八剌哈孫 *Ha-la-ba-la-ha-sun*. Thus the present name of *Khara-balgasun* (see note 108) was in use even

---
Yüan shi reports in chap. lxiv, where a separate article is devoted to this river *Luan* connecting Shang-tu with the sea. Corn could be carried on it up to Shang-tu. M. Polo states that the Sanghin river is ascended by merchants from the sea. The Hun ho may be navigable even now in its lower course, but for trade is of little importance. From the Lu-kou bridge upward, rafts are occasionally met with on the river, but boats are seen only after the rainy season at the ferries. In winter time they are replaced by miserable bridges.

112. *Cf.* Klaproth in *Nouveau Journal Asiatique*, tom. xi, p. 335. Even Col. Yule, who is always so sagacious and cautious in commenting, has adopted this view; see *Cathay*, etc. p. 260.

in the Mongol times. Perhaps Rashid's statement, that in former times the emperors used to live at Chúchú, points to these facts recorded in the Chinese annals. The only feasible objection to my view would appear to be the distance between Fu chou and Se-ma-lin being nearly 30 English miles; for Rashid places his Semali near Chúchú. But the ancient road to Shang-tu passed indeed, as we have seen, near Si-ma lin and through Fu chou.

In the ancient Chinese itineraries, a branch of this western road to Shang-tu, just spoken of, is alluded to as striking off from the station of *T'ung-mu* (see note 104) to the north, and joining afterwards the first or direct road to Shang-tu. This is the road which even now connects this station with the city of 赤城 *Ch'i-ch'eng* and leads to the gate *Tu-shi k'ou*. Chi-ch'eng did not yet exist in the Mongol times.

Let us turn now to the third road to Shang-tu, which lay by 古北口 *Ku-pei k'ou*. This road, according to the ancient itineraries, was used generally by the officers in the suite of the emperors, and for conveying the baggage of the emperor. No other details are found in the *Shang tu yi ch'eng k'ao* regarding the Ku-pei k'ou road, which I am inclined to identify with Rashid's third road, "which takes the direction of the pass of *Sengling* (other readings are Siking, and Sengking), beyond which you find only prairies and plains abounding in game until you reach Kaiminfu."

Ku-pei k'ou is an ancient name. This defile, about 70 English miles to the north-west of Peking and crossed by the Great wall, was known by the same name as early as the 10th century (*Liao shi*, geographical part), and is mentioned repeatedly in the Chinese annals of the Mongol period. But Rashid's Sengling has no resemblance to *Ku-pei k'ou* There is a mountain range 新開嶺 *Sin-k'ai ling*, marked on Chinese maps near Ku-pei k'ou, and spoken of also in the *Ji hia*, chap. cliii, fol. 15. This name sounds like Rashid's Sengling, and a bold commentator would perhaps venture an identification. But after passing Ku-pei k'ou, the traveller going to the north has to cross much higher mountains before he reaches the Mongolian steppes. I propose another more plausible explanation of Rashid's account.

The great chain of mountains, separating Manchuria from Mongolia and marked on our maps as *Khingan* range, stretches at first from north to south, and then turning to the west, separates the plateau of Mongolia from China proper. *Khingan* is not a Chinese but a Manchu name, which was probably also in use during the Kin and Mongol periods. In Chinese books this range is termed 興安嶺 *Hing-an ling* (pronounced *Sing-an ling* in the northern Chinese dialect).[113] I feel tolerably

---

113. *Cf. Chêng te fu chi*, section on hills and rivers.

certain that this is the word Rashid wished to render by Sengling.[114] *Ling* in Chinese means "a range of mountains." Proceeding from Kupei k'ou northward, the traveller has to traverse the Khingan range,[115] beyond which he has before him the vast prairies of Mongolia. *Cf.* Col. Prejewalsky's *Monoglia and the country of the Tanguts*, 1875 (in Russian) pp, 72, 73.

Finally I may be allowed to say a few words regarding the palace *Langtin*, built as the Persian historiographer reports, on the eastern side of Shang-tu. The correctness of this statement can also be proved from Chinese sources. According to the *Shang tu yi ch'eng k'ao*, there were two 凉亭 *Liang-t'ing* or "cool pavilions (palaces)," one 50 *li* east of Shang-tu, the other 150 *li* west of the summer residence.

---

114. Rashid's proper names used with respect to China and Mongolia are not always Mongol terms. Although his information was drawn, it seems, only from Mongol sources, we find frequently in his records Chinese names quoted, *e. g.* Daidu, Kaiminfu, and Lantin.
115. Nearly 4000 feet high (Prejewalsky).

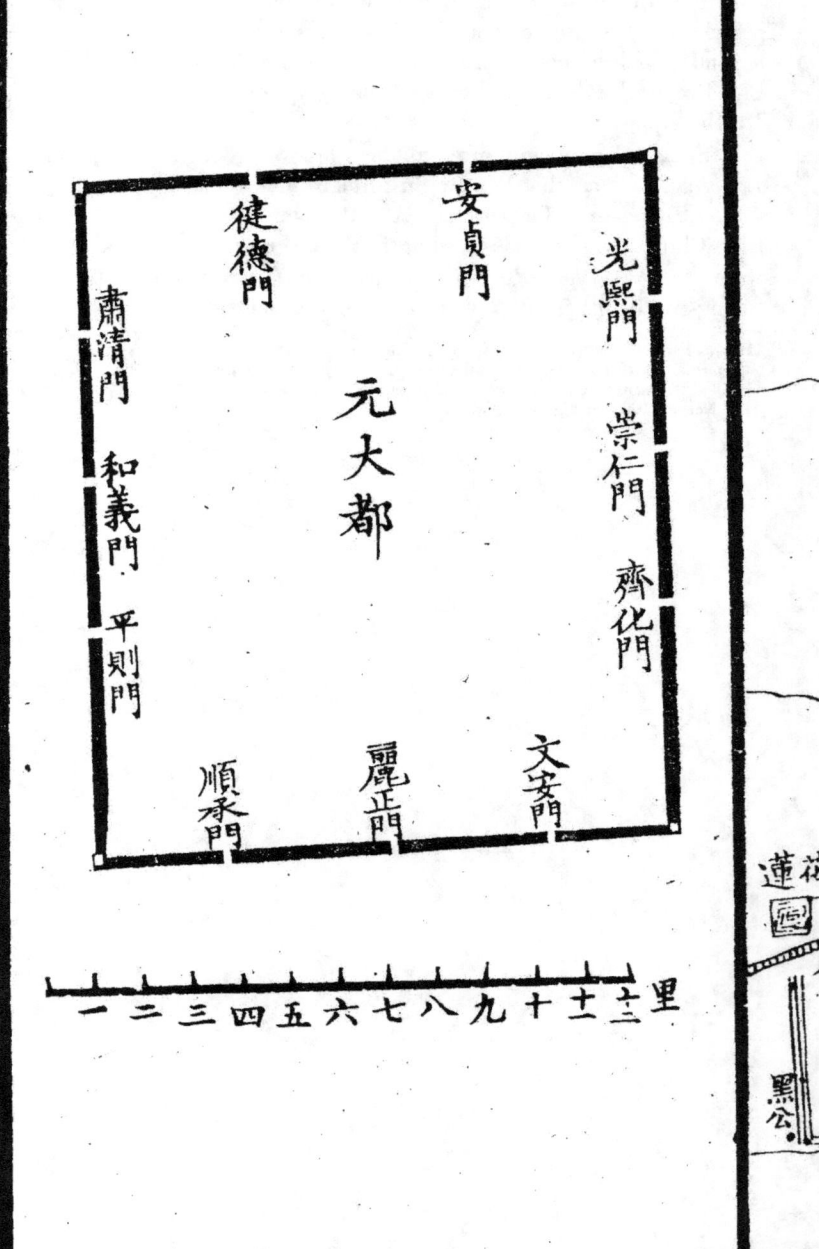

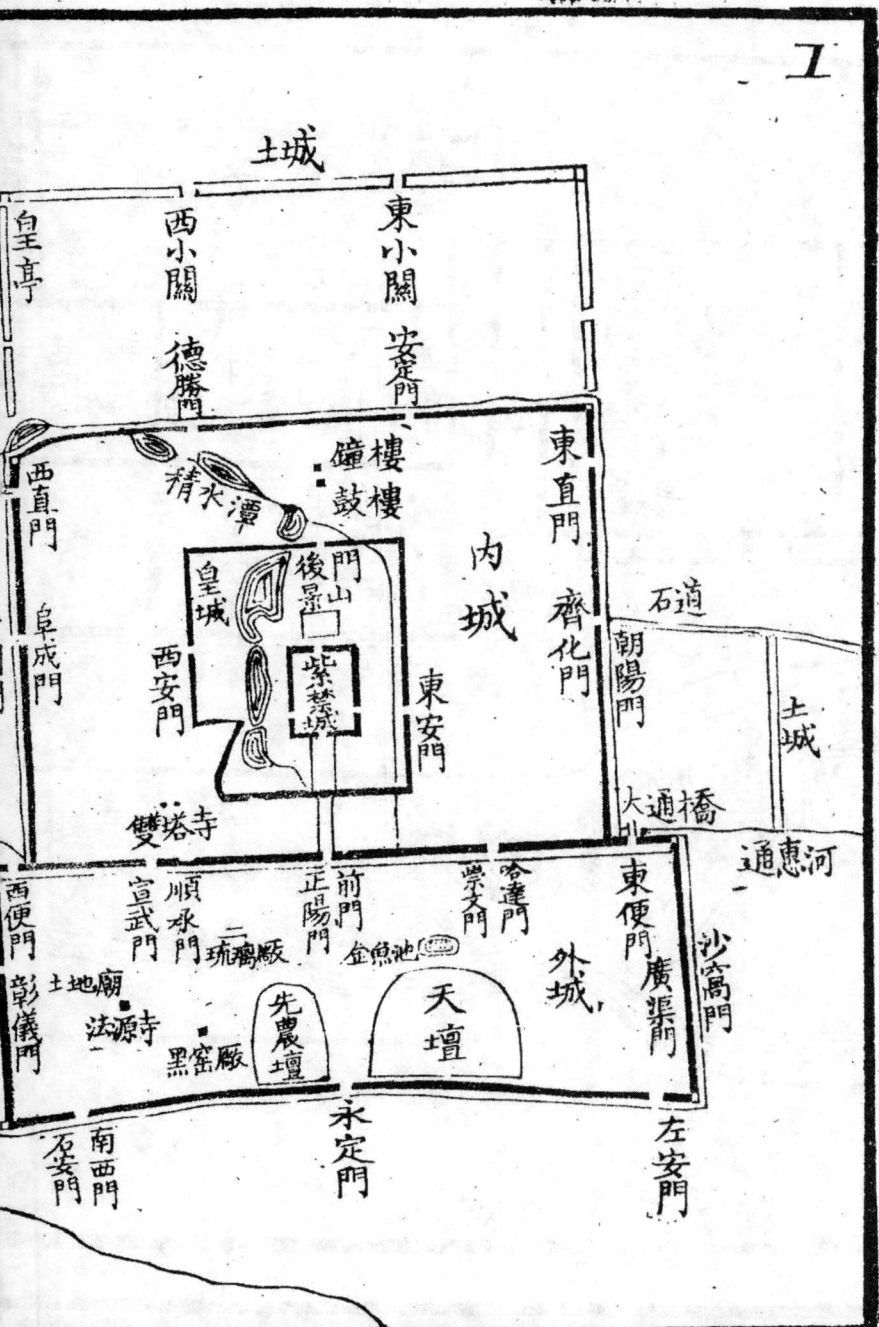

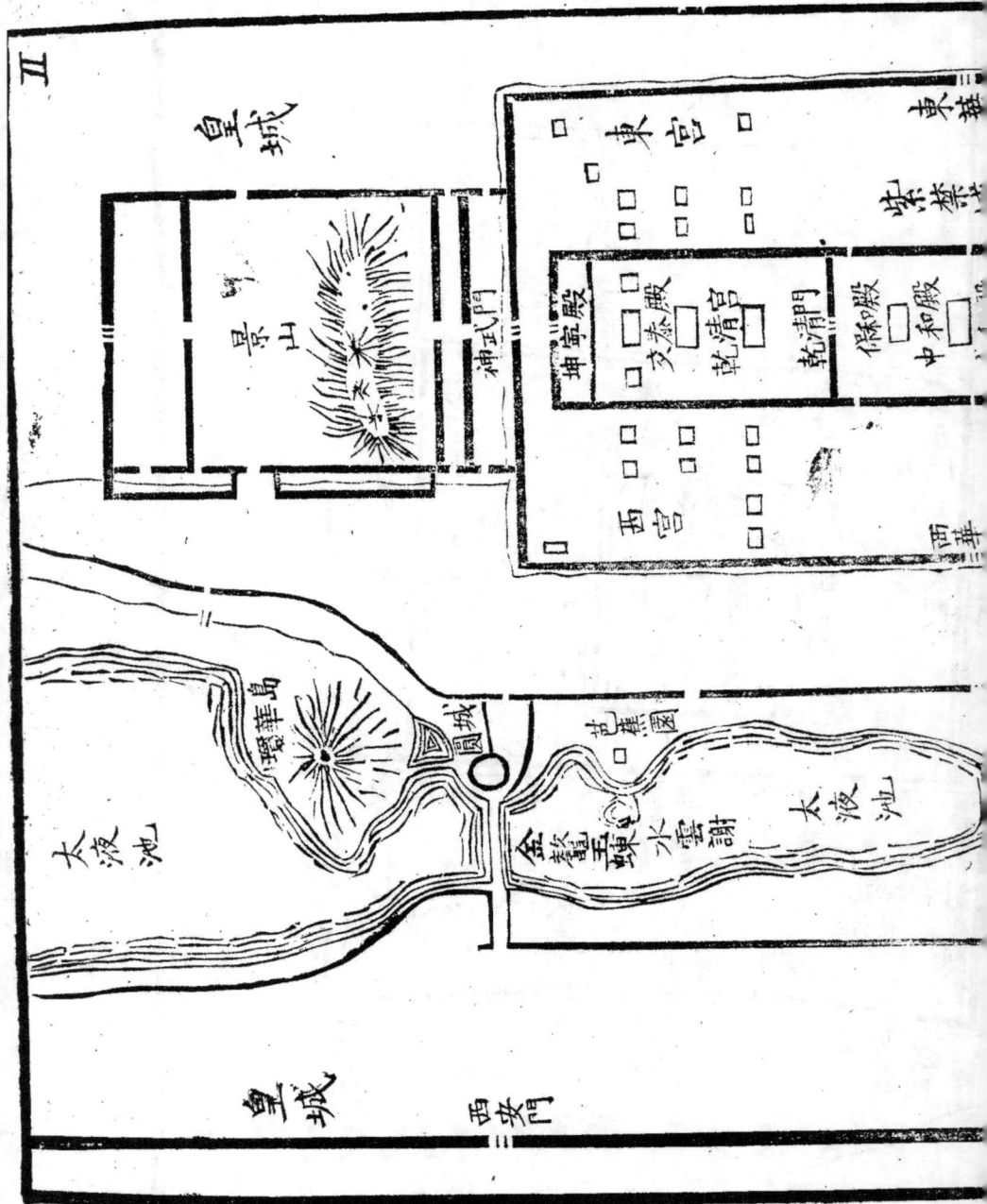

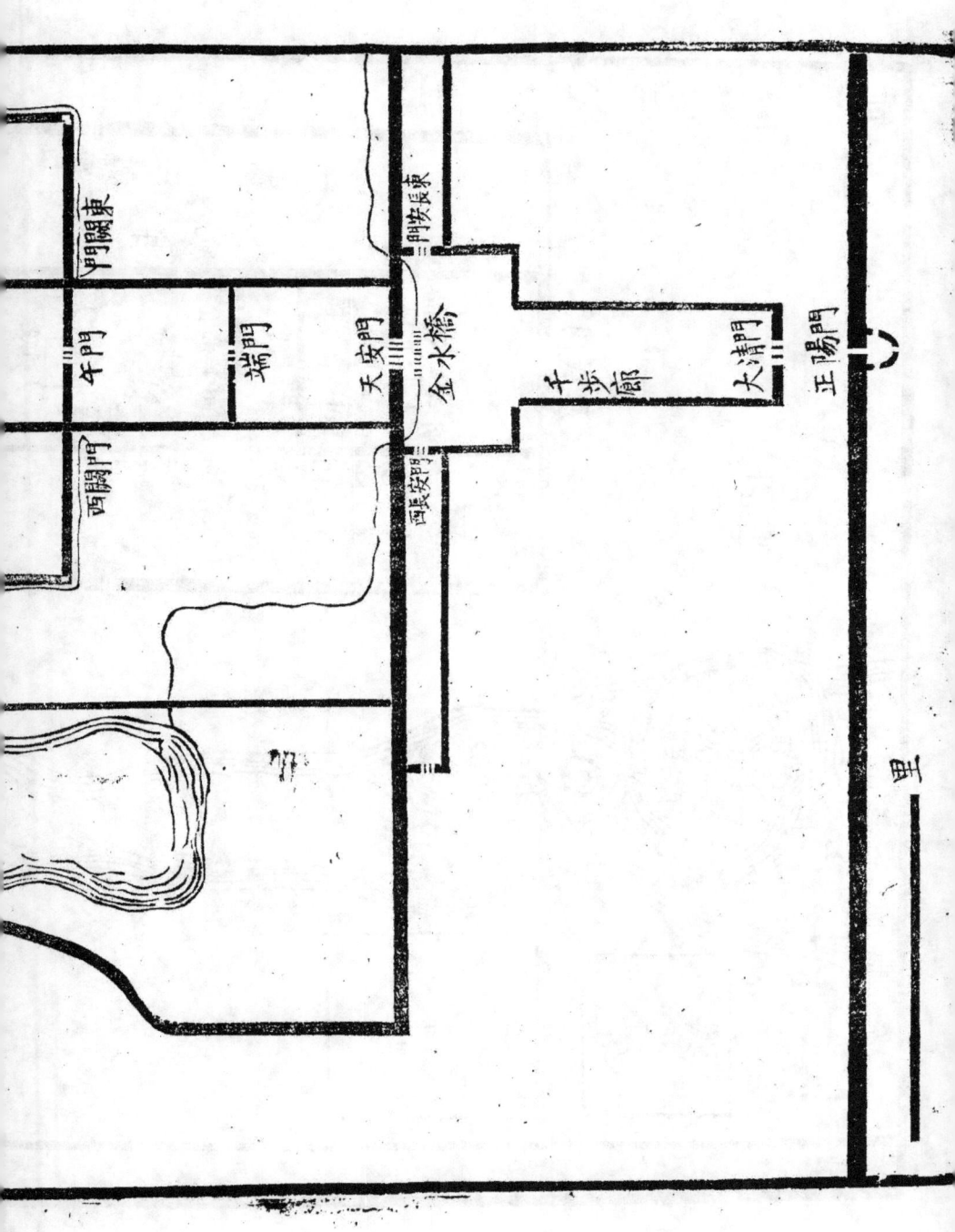

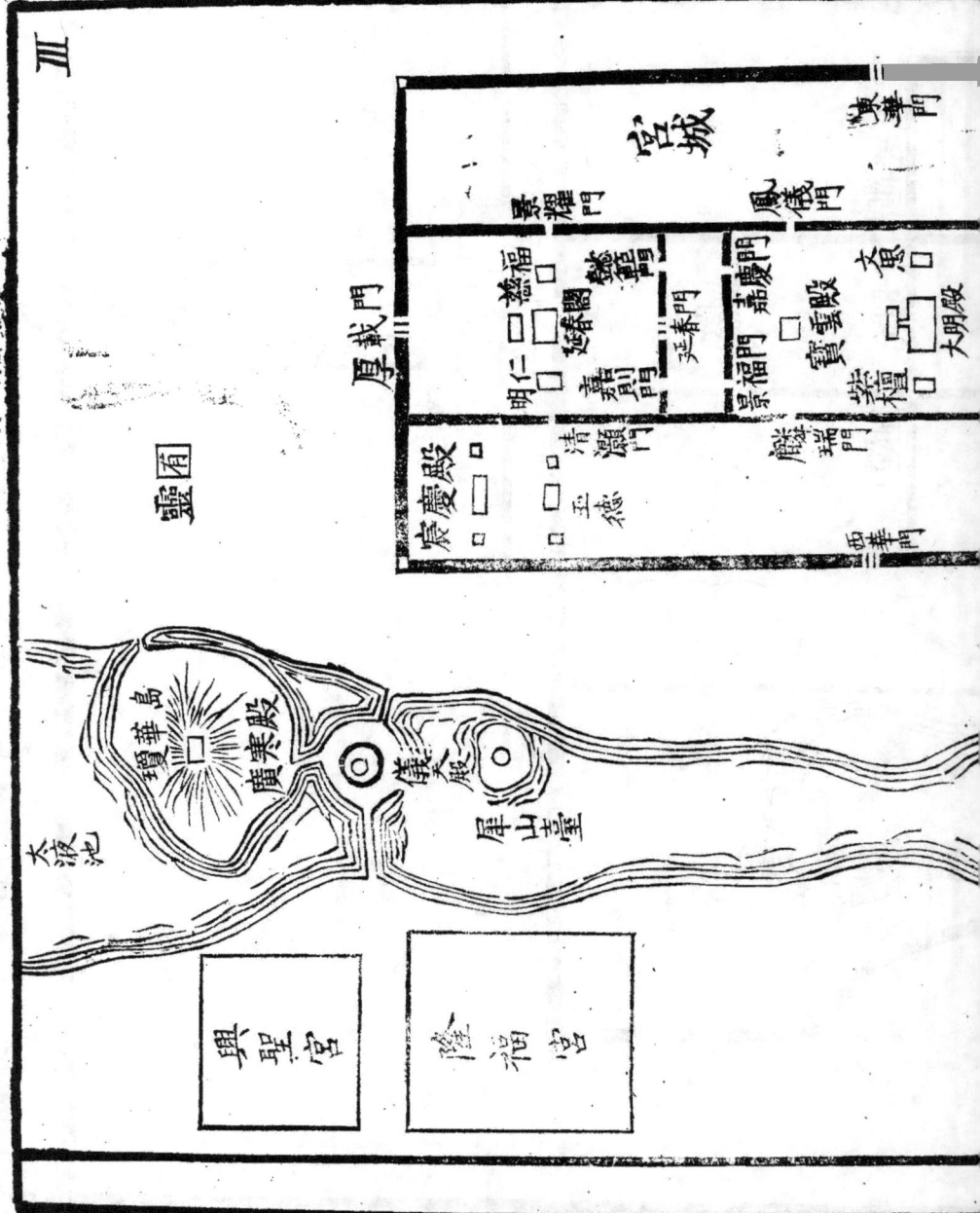

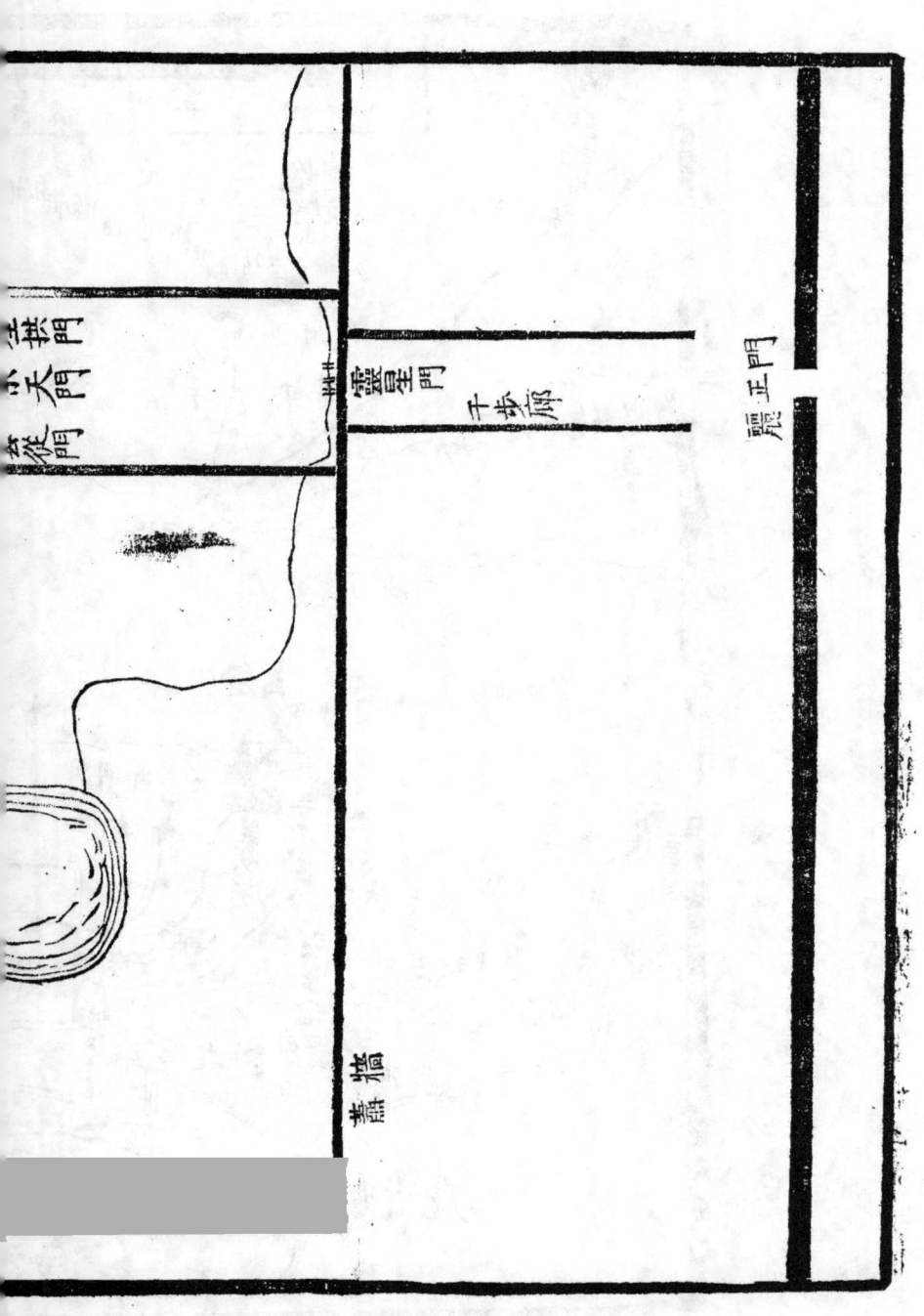

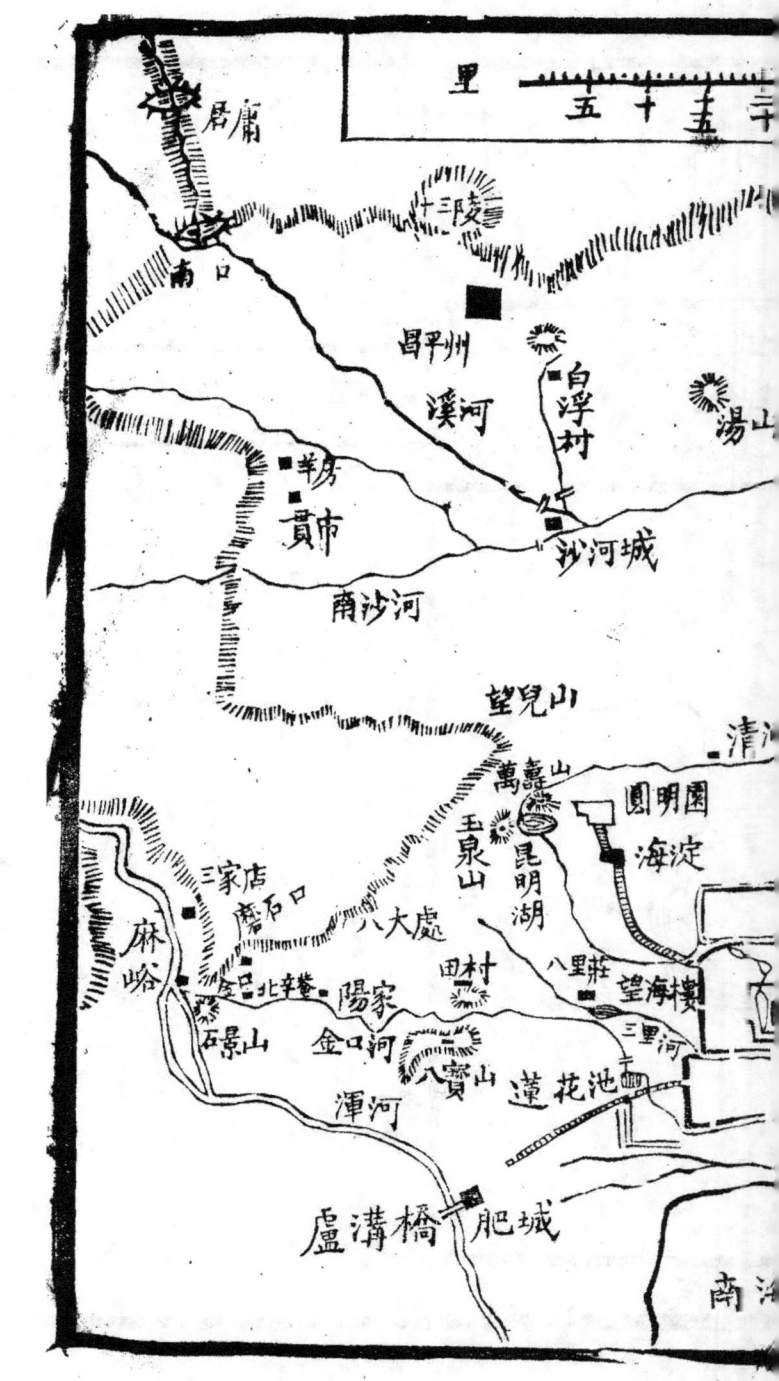

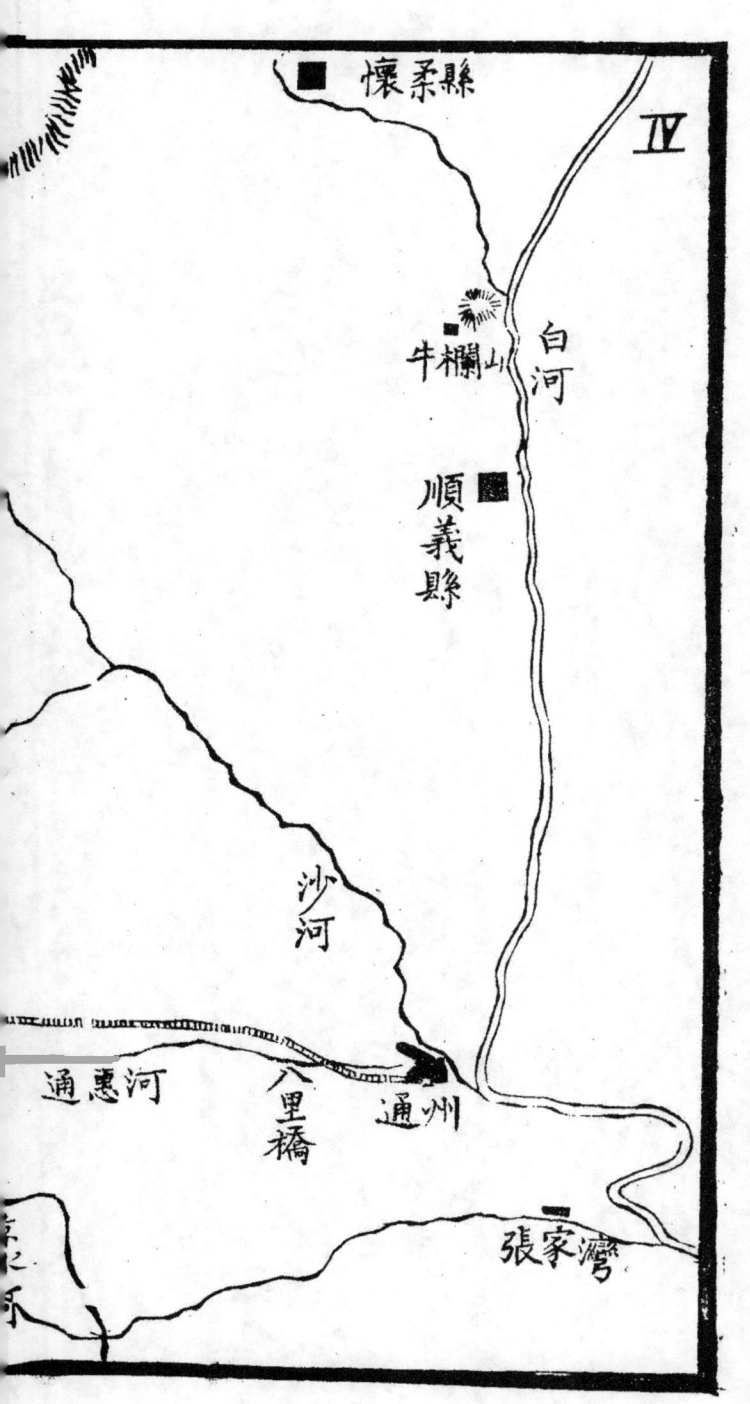

Ebenfalls im SEVERUS Verlag erhältlich:

Emil Bretschneider
History of European Botanical Discoveries in China
SEVERUS 2011 / 648 Seiten / 69,50 Euro
ISBN 978-3-86347-165-1

"It has been attempted in the following pages to supply the want of a work of reference, in which botanists dealing with Chinese plants preserved in European herbariums might find some particulars regarding the history of these collections, of which the labels affixed to the herbarium specimens generally give only an imperfect account."

Emil Bretschneider (1833–1901) became famous among researchers for his valuable contributions to the field of sinology. His versatile approach – he was a physician and botanist as well as a sinologist – and his familiarity with Chinese literature distinguished him from his colleagues, many of whom were unable to read sources firsthand.

Combining his abilities in botany and sinology, Bretschneider comprises an extensive history of Chinese plants and how they found their way to Europe. From the earliest accounts by Marco Polo, to the groundbreaking work of Carl Linnaeus, to the period of the Opium wars between England and China, this volume covers the works of European botanists up until 1860. Bretschneider does not limit his scope to China proper, but includes Mongolia, Tibet, Korea, and other regions, making this a uniquely comprehensive guide to European research on Asian plants.

www.severus-verlag.de

Bisher im SEVERUS Verlag erschienen:

Achelis. Th. Die Entwicklung der Ehe * Die Religionen der Naturvölker im Umriß, Reihe ReligioSus Band V * **Andreas-Salomé, Lou** Rainer Maria Rilke * **Arenz, Karl** Die Entdeckungsreisen in Nord- und Mittelafrika von Richardson, Overweg, Barth und Vogel * **Aretz, Gertrude (Hrsg)** Napoleon I - Briefe an Frauen * **Ashburn, P.M** The ranks of death. A Medical History of the Conquest of America * **Avenarius, Richard** Kritik der reinen Erfahrung * Kritik der reinen Erfahrung, Zweiter Teil * **Beneke, Otto** Von unehrlichen Leuten: Kulturhistorische Studien und Geschichten aus vergangenen Tagen deutscher Gewerbe und Dienste * **Berneker, Erich** Graf Leo Tolstoi * **Bernstorff, Graf Johann Heinrich** Erinnerungen und Briefe * **Bie, Oscar** Franz Schubert - Sein Leben und sein Werk * **Binder, Julius** Grundlegung zur Rechtsphilosophie. Mit einem Extratext zur Rechtsphilosophie Hegels * **Bliedner, Arno** Schiller. Eine pädagogische Studie * **Birt, Theodor** Frauen der Antike * **Blümner, Hugo** Fahrendes Volk im Altertum * **Boos, Heinrich** Geschichte der Freimaurerei. Ein Beitrag zur Kultur- und Literatur-Geschichte des 18. Jahrhunderts * **Brahm, Otto** Das deutsche Ritterdrama des achtzehnten Jahrhunderts: Studien über Joseph August von Törring, seine Vorgänger und Nachfolger * **Brandes, Georg** Moderne Geister: Literarische Bildnisse aus dem 19. Jahrhundert. * **Braun, Lily** Lebenssucher * **Braun, Ferdinand** Drahtlose Telegraphie durch Wasser und Luft * **Brunnemann, Karl** Maximilian Robespierre - Ein Lebensbild nach zum Teil noch unbenutzten Quellen * **Büdinger, Max** Don Carlos Haft und Tod insbesondere nach den Auffassungen seiner Familie * **Burkamp, Wilhelm** Wirklichkeit und Sinn. Die objektive Gewordenheit des Sinns in der sinnfreien Wirklichkeit * **Caemmerer, Rudolf Karl Fritz** Die Entwicklung der strategischen Wissenschaft im 19. Jahrhundert * **Casper, Johann Ludwig** Handbuch der gerichtlich-medizinischen Leichen-Diagnostik: Thanatologischer Teil, Bd. 1 * Bd. 2 * **Cronau, Rudolf** Drei Jahrhunderte deutschen Lebens in Amerika. Eine Geschichte der Deutschen in den Vereinigten Staaten * **Cunow, Heinrich** Geschichte und Kultur des Inkareiches * **Cushing, Harvey** The life of Sir William Osler, Volume 1 * The life of Sir William Osler, Volume 2 * **Dahlke, Paul** Buddhismus als Religion und Moral, Reihe ReligioSus Band IV * **Dühren, Eugen** Der Marquis de Sade und seine Zeit. in Beitrag zur Kultur- und Sittengeschichte des 18. Jahrhunderts. Mit besonderer Beziehung auf die Lehre von der Psychopathia Sexualis * **Eckstein, Friedrich** Alte, unnennbare Tage. Erinnerungen aus siebzig Lehr- und Wanderjahren * Erinnerungen an Anton Bruckner * **Eiselsberg, Anton Freiherr von** Lebensweg eines Chirurgen * **Eloesser, Arthur** Thomas Mann - sein Leben und Werk * **Elsenhans, Theodor** Fries und Kant. Ein Beitrag zur Geschichte und zur systematischen Grundlegung der Erkenntnistheorie. * **Engel, Eduard** Shakespeare * Lord Byron. Eine Autobiographie nach Tagebüchern und Briefen. * **Ewald, Oscar** Nietzsches Lehre in ihren Grundbegriffen * Die französische Aufklärungsphilosophie * **Ferenczi, Sandor** Hysterie und Pathoneurosen * **Fichte, Immanuel Hermann** Die Idee der Persönlichkeit und der individuellen Fortdauer * **Fourier, Jean Baptiste Joseph Baron** Die Auflösung der bestimmten Gleichungen * **Frazer, James George** Totemism and Exogamy. A Treatise on Certain Early Forms of Superstition and Society * **Frey, Adolf** Albrecht von Haller und seine Bedeutung für die deutsche Literatur * **Frimmel, Theodor von** Beethoven Studien I. Beethovens äußere Erscheinung * Beethoven Studien II. Bausteine zu einer Lebensgeschichte des Meisters * **Fülleborn, Friedrich** Über eine medizinische Studienreise nach Panama, Westindien und den Vereinigten Staaten * **Gmelin, Johann Georg** Quousque? Beiträge zur soziologischen Rechtfindung * **Goette, Alexander** Holbeins Totentanz und seine Vorbilder * **Goldstein, Eugen** Canalstrahlen * **Graebner, Fritz** Das Weltbild der Primitiven: Eine Untersuchung der Urformen weltanschaulichen Denkens bei Naturvölkern * **Griesinger, Wilhelm** Handbuch der speciellen Pathologie und Therapie: Infectionskrankheiten * **Griesser, Luitpold** Nietzsche und Wagner - neue Beiträge zur Geschichte und Psychologie ihrer Freundschaft * **Hanstein, Adalbert von** Die Frauen in der Geschichte des Deutschen Geisteslebens des 18. und 19. Jahrhunderts * **Hartmann, Franz** Die Medizin des Theophrastus Paracelsus von Hohenheim * **Heller, August** Geschichte der Physik von Aristoteles bis auf die neueste Zeit. Bd. 1: Von Aristoteles bis Galilei * **Helmholtz, Hermann von** Reden und Vorträge, Bd. 1 * Reden und Vorträge, Bd. 2 * **Henker, Otto** Einführung in die Brillenlehre * **Henne am Rhyn, Otto** Aus Loge und Welt: Freimaurerische und kulturgeschichtliche Aufsätze * **Jahn, Ulrich** Die deutschen Opfergebräuche bei Ackerbau und Viehzucht. Ein Beitrag zur Deutschen Mythologie und Altertumskunde * **Kalkoff, Paul** Ulrich von Hutten und die Reformation. Eine kritische Geschichte seiner wichtigsten Lebenszeit und der Ent-

scheidungsjahre der Reformation (1517 - 1523), Reihe ReligioSus Band I * **Kaufmann, Max** Heines Liebesleben * **Kautsky, Karl** Terrorismus und Kommunismus: Ein Beitrag zur Naturgeschichte der Revolution * **Kerschensteiner, Georg** Theorie der Bildung * **Kotelmann, Ludwig** Gesundheitspflege im Mittelalter. Kulturgeschichtliche Studien nach Predigten des 13., 14. und 15. Jahrhunderts * **Klein, Wilhelm** Geschichte der Griechischen Kunst - Erster Band: Die Griechische Kunst bis Myron * **Krömeke, Franz** Friedrich Wilhelm Sertürner - Entdecker des Morphiums * **Külz, Ludwig** Tropenarzt im afrikanischen Busch * **Leimbach, Karl Alexander** Untersuchungen über die verschiedenen Moralsysteme * **Liliencron, Rochus von / Müllenhoff, Karl** Zur Runenlehre. Zwei Abhandlungen * **Mach, Ernst** Die Principien der Wärmelehre * **Mackenzie, William Leslie** Health and Disease * **Maurer, Konrad** Island von seiner ersten Entdeckung bis zum Untergange des Freistaats * **Mausbach, Joseph** Die Ethik des heiligen Augustinus. Erster Band: Die sittliche Ordnung und ihre Grundlagen * **Mauthner, Fritz** Die drei Bilder der Welt - ein sprachkritischer Versuch * **Meissner, Franz Hermann** Arnold Böcklin * Meyer, **Elard Hugo** Indogermanische Mythen, Bd. 1: Gandharven-Kentauren * **Müller, Adam** Versuche einer neuen Theorie des Geldes * **Müller, Conrad** Alexander von Humboldt und das Preußische Königshaus. Briefe aus den Jahren 1835-1857 * **Naumann, Friedrich** Freiheitskämpfe * **Oettingen, Arthur von** Die Schule der Physik * **Ossipow, Nikolai** Tolstois Kindheitserinnerungen. Ein Beitrag zu Freuds Libidotheorie * **Ostwald, Wilhelm** Erfinder und Entdecker * **Peters, Carl** Die deutsche Emin-Pascha-Expedition * **Poetter, Friedrich Christoph** Logik * **Popken, Minna** Im Kampf um die Welt des Lichts. Lebenserinnerungen und Bekenntnisse einer Ärztin * **Prutz, Hans** Neue Studien zur Geschichte der Jungfrau von Orléans * **Rank, Otto** Psychoanalytische Beiträge zur Mythenforschung. Gesammelte Studien aus den Jahren 1912 bis 1914. * **Ree, Paul Johannes** Peter Candid * **Rohr, Moritz von** Joseph Fraunhofers Leben, Leistungen und Wirksamkeit * **Rubinstein, Susanna** Ein individualistischer Pessimist: Beitrag zur Würdigung Philipp Mainländers * Eine Trias von Willensmetaphysikern: Populär-philosophische Essays * **Sachs, Eva** Die fünf platonischen Körper: Zur Geschichte der Mathematik und der Elementenlehre Platons und der Pythagoreer * **Scheidemann, Philipp** Memoiren eines Sozialdemokraten, Erster Band * Memoiren eines Sozialdemokraten, Zweiter Band * **Schleich, Carl Ludwig** Erinnerungen an Strindberg nebst Nachrufen für Ehrlich und von Bergmann * Das Ich und die Dämonien * **Schlösser, Rudolf** Rameaus Neffe - Studien und Untersuchungen zur Einführung in Goethes Übersetzung des Diderotschen Dialogs * **Schweitzer, Christoph** Reise nach Java und Ceylon (1675-1682). Reisebeschreibungen von deutschen Beamten und Kriegsleuten im Dienst der niederländischen West- und Ostindischen Kompagnien 1602 - 1797. * **Schweitzer, Philipp** Island - Land und Leute * **Sommerlad, Theo** Die soziale Wirksamkeit der Hohenzollern * **Stein, Heinrich von** Giordano Bruno. Gedanken über seine Lehre und sein Leben * **Strache, Hans** Der Eklektizismus des Antiochus von Askalon * **Sulger-Gebing, Emil** Goethe und Dante * **Thiersch, Hermann** Ludwig I von Bayern und die Georgia Augusta * Pro Samothrake * **Tyndall, John** Die Wärme betrachtet als eine Art der Bewegung, Bd. 1 * Die Wärme betrachtet als eine Art der Bewegung, Bd. 2 * **Virchow, Rudolf** Vier Reden über Leben und Kranksein * **Vollmann, Franz** Über das Verhältnis der späteren Stoa zur Sklaverei im römischen Reiche * **Volkmer, Franz** Das Verhältnis von Geist und Körper im Menschen (Seele und Leib) nach Cartesius * **Wachsmuth, Curt** Das alte Griechenland im neuen * **Weber, Paul** Beiträge zu Dürers Weltanschauung * **Wecklein, Nikolaus** Textkritische Studien zu den griechischen Tragikern * **Weinhold, Karl** Die heidnische Totenbestattung in Deutschland * **Wellhausen, Julius** Israelitische und Jüdische Geschichte, Reihe ReligioSus Band VI *ated**Wellmann, Max** Die pneumatische Schule bis auf Archigenes - in ihrer Entwickelung dargestellt * **Wernher, Adolf** Die Bestattung der Toten in Bezug auf Hygiene, geschichtliche Entwicklung und gesetzliche Bestimmungen * **Weygandt, Wilhelm** Abnorme Charaktere in der dramatischen Literatur. Shakespeare - Goethe - Ibsen - Gerhart Hauptmann * **Wlassak, Moriz** Zum römischen Provinzialprozeß * **Wulffen, Erich** Kriminalpädagogik: Ein Erziehungsbuch * **Wundt, Wilhelm** Reden und Aufsätze * **Zallinger, Otto** Die Ringgaben bei der Heirat und das Zusammengeben im mittelalterlich-deutschem Recht * **Zoozmann, Richard** Hans Sachs und die Reformation - In Gedichten und Prosastücken, Reihe ReligioSus Band III

www.severus-verlag.de

www.ingramcontent.com/pod-product-compliance
Lightning Source LLC
Chambersburg PA
CBHW051616230426
43668CB00013B/2131